Scribners

Five Generations in Publishing

CHARLES SCRIBNER III

LYONS
PRESS

Essex, Connecticut

An imprint of Globe Pequot, the trade division of
The Rowman & Littlefield Publishing Group, Inc.
4501 Forbes Blvd., Ste. 200
Lanham, MD 20706
www.rowman.com

Distributed by NATIONAL BOOK NETWORK

British Library Cataloguing in Publication Information available

Library of Congress Cataloging-in-Publication Data
Names: Scribner, Charles, 1951- author.
Title: Scribners : five generations in publishing / Charles Scribner III.
Description: Essex, Connecticut : Lyons Press, [2023] | Includes index.
Identifiers: LCCN 2023017415 (print) | LCCN 2023017416 (ebook) | ISBN
    9781493079971 (hardcover) | ISBN 9781493079988 (epub)
Subjects: LCSH: Charles Scribner's Sons—History. | Charles Scribner's Sons—
    Biography. | Publishers and publishing—United States—Biography. | Authors and
    publishers—United States—History.
Classification: LCC Z473.C46 S37 2023 (print) | LCC Z473.C46 (ebook) | DDC
    070.5092 [B]—dc23/eng/20230526
LC record available at https://lccn.loc.gov/2023017415
LC ebook record available at https://lccn.loc.gov/2023017416

For my grandchildren:

Elizabeth, Charlotte, and Charles

Contents

Scribner Building, 597 Fifth Avenue, pastel by Kamil Kubik (1983)

Reading is a means of thinking with another person's mind; it forces you to stretch your own. . . . For learning purposes there is no substitute for one human mind meeting another on the page of a well-written book.

—Charles Scribner Jr.

PREFACE

I have spent most of my life—in and out of publishing—as a professional son. If it runs in the family, as this ensuing tale may suggest, it is a role I still maintain even now as a grandfather to the seventh Charles in succession; redundancy as well as nepotism is a family tradition. In this spirit, I owe the reader a note of confession. What I offer here is a personal account of five successive Charleses in the same house. Why did I write this book? Because Michelle Rapkin, the brilliant and beloved editor of my past three books, told me upon finishing my most recent, *Sacred Muse: A Preface to Christian Art and Music* (2023), that I must; she argued that if I didn't commit to printing the following stories—those told to me by my father and those I experienced myself—they would disappear forever.

Toward the end of his life, my father wrote (or more precisely, dictated, as part of an oral history) a gem of memoir, *In the Company of Writers* (1990), followed by a book of essays, *In the Web of Ideas* (1993). I commend them to all readers who love books and what he called "the life of the mind." But my dad was too modest—and too discreet—to include all the stories he had shared with me. I have no such reticence, for I am writing first for an audience of three: my grandchildren, Elizabeth, Charlotte, and Charles, to whom I dedicate this book. If others beyond these youngest Scribners find it of interest, that is icing on the cake.

Chapter 1

The Founder

When I look back at 175 years of our family publishing history beginning in 1846, I find myself drawn back—ceaselessly, "against the current"—to a novel that I first read as a teenager for an assignment in English class, a book that for the ensuing half century I have read more times than any other in my life and watched on-screen in four successive films: *The Great Gatsby*. If that title seems obvious in hindsight, it was far from preordained. Indeed I wonder now whether I would ever have read it—much less been assigned it—if its publisher, my great-grandfather, had been more deferential to its young author, F. Scott Fitzgerald.

In the flush of creativity, Fitzgerald wrote to his Scribner editor, Maxwell Perkins: "I feel I have enormous power in me now, more than I've ever had in a way, but it works so fitfully and with so many bogeys because I've talked so much and not lived enough within myself to develop the necessary self-reliance. Also I don't know anyone who has used up so much personal experience as I have at 27." Perkins, for his part, had grave reservations about the proposed title "Among the Ash Heaps and Millionaires" and suggested that Fitzgerald return to "The Great Gatsby," which he called effective and suggestive. He also commissioned at this early date—seven months before the author completed his manuscript—the most famous jacket painting of the past century.

Fitzgerald continued to revise his draft from September to October, "working at high pressure to finish," he wrote in his ledger. In November 1924 he mailed the manuscript to Perkins with a new title, "Trimalchio in West Egg." He was to run through several others—"Trimalchio," "Gold Hatted Gatsby," "Gatsby," "The High-Bouncing Lover," and "On the Road to West Egg"—before Perkins's steady favorite, "The Great Gatsby," was restored in time for publication. Most of the final revising was done directly on the printed galley proofs, which Fitzgerald treated almost as a clean typescript (in fact those uncorrected galleys, titled "Trimalchio," were published several years ago, as if a distinct novel). Then, just three weeks before publication (April 10, 1925) the nervous author cabled his editor from Paris: "Crazy about title 'Under the Red, White, and Blue.'" But fortunately it was too late to change the title and the book was spared the fate of sounding like a George M. Cohan song. I cannot imagine any of those preferred titles by the author on the cover of the greatest-selling classic in our history.

But I'm getting ahead of myself—nothing unusual. I've already jumped over two generations of Scribners to rush headlong into the Jazz Age. Our house was almost eighty years old when overtaken by this onslaught of timeless youth. I should start at the beginning—a sound if not novel idea.

The history of our publishing house begins in 1846 with a partnership between the twenty-five-year-old Charles Scribner and a merchant named Isaac Baker, a friend of Scribner's father, Uriah Rogers Scribner, who was himself a successful merchant in New York City, living in a townhouse at 751 Broadway between Eighth Street and Astor Place, today an apartment complex near New York University. One of ten children, Charles had been born in Fairfield County, Connecticut, where his family first settled in 1680. The founder of that American branch of Scribners—then spelled "Scrivener"—was Benjamin, who sailed over from England in 1679 and married Hannah Crampton in Norwalk,

Connecticut, in 1680. The surname means a professional clerk or "scribe," like Herman Melville's famous short-story character Bartleby, the Scrivener—a fitting one for a family that would eventually wind up in the company of writers.

The first Charles in our long line of seven (so far) graduated from the Lawrenceville School in New Jersey. He attended New York University for a year, a short stroll from his home, before heading back to New Jersey to graduate from Princeton—then called the College of New Jersey—in the class of 1840. He was all of nineteen. A few months ago, I happened to find in the Scribner archives at Princeton a college paper that he wrote about the religious tensions in the Holy Land. It was titled "The Arab." *Plus ça change.* But of still greater revelation was a letter he wrote to his mother from Lawrenceville in July of 1837 (obviously there were no long summer vacations in those days, which may explain the speedy graduations). Even more stunning than his exquisite penmanship is the maturity and expressiveness of his prose at age sixteen—and the intensity of his religious convictions.

My very dear Mother, I could have called you by this endearing name one week ago because I felt myself bound to you by the strongest ties of filial affection, but now in addition to this I can call you my Dear Mother because I have the full assurances that you are a child of God and, Oh!, the love which I now feel for my Saviour increases my love for one whom I firmly believe has this same love for him and I hope in a much stronger degree. Oh my dear mother, I think that I can cherish the hope that my heart is changed, not by any good acts of my own but by the wonderful and amazing love of a Saviour who was so kind and so compassionate to poor and unworthy sinners as to take upon himself our sins and bear in our stead the death of the cross.

The letter continues in this vein for several more pages—a far cry from the text messages of teenagers today. He was young enough then to be my grandson, yet I felt I was reading a letter from a wise elder. As Einstein proved, time is indeed relative.

Charles had first planned a career in the law, but because of his frail health he was obliged to take a trip abroad and, upon his return, to choose something less strenuous. He chose publishing as a more congenial profession. I wonder whether the relative hardship of those two professions would still be appraised in the same way. Would any wise doctor prescribe a career in publishing today?

The location selected for the budding venture was an unused chapel in the old Brick Church (then called the Brick Meeting House) on the corner of Nassau Street and Park Row, across from City Hall in downtown Manhattan. Today it is the site of the old New York Times Building, now part of Pace University. In those days the area was an informal headquarters of the book trade; no doubt it was also comforting to the religious twenty-five-year-old to set up shop within the hallowed walls of his family's parish church. At that time, the idea to start up an independent publishing company—that is, a company devoted solely to book *publishing*—was something of an innovation. Most of the established houses had either grown out of printing plants, following the noble tradition of the sixteenth-century Plantin Press in Antwerp, or were offshoots of retail bookshops. On the one hand, a printer might venture into publishing to provide work for his presses; on the other, a bookseller might become a part-time publisher to supply extra books to sell in his store.

There were practical advantages to Scribner's decision to be more specialized. Since his new firm was able to start business without having to worry about the costs of keeping a manufacturing plant humming with presses, it was possible to focus from day one on the work of new authors, particularly American authors, without having to compete with others in publishing reprints of

the best-selling writers from England—Sir Walter Scott, Trol-
lope, Dickens, Lord Macaulay, and the Victorian poets. In short,
the first Charles set out to originate works and discover fresh
talent. It has remained the guiding policy since 1846. I might add
that in the nineteenth century the more common occupation of
American publishers—publishing reprints of English authors—
was akin to intellectual property thieves today; American publishers were viewed by their English counterparts as not much higher
than pirates on the high sea. There was as yet no such thing as
international copyright protection. Each pirate for himself.

According to modern tastes none of the early titles from
Baker & Scribner would be candidates for the bestseller lists. The
roster was heavy with theological treatises, most of them impen-
etrable today. Charles's grandfather Matthew Scribner graduated
from Yale in 1775 and had a long career as an ordained Congregational minister, so Calvinism remained the favorite flavor
on the Scribner book menu. Grandfather surely smiled from on
high. The first book published in 1846 was an austere tome titled
The Puritans and Their Principles. The author, Reverend Edwin
Hall, was the minister of the Congregational church in Norwalk,
Connecticut, the Scribners' original hometown, which I visited
a few summers ago and where I discovered "Scribner Avenue." I
climbed the street pole out of filial piety. More practical, I found
the first edition on the Internet and purchased it. In this devoutly
Calvinist book based on a series of lectures, Hall had nothing
good to say about the Catholic Church (my adoptive faith) or
even Episcopalians—especially their bishops. The following passage, which I read aloud at the annual dinner of the New England
Society some twenty years ago when accepting an award, sums up
the tone—and tome:

> *O what emotions often fill my soul, when, on the very soil on*
> *which the early fathers of New England trod, and looking*
> *abroad over the hills and waters on which they once looked,*

*and while walking amid their graves, I think of the hand of
God so dearly revealed; and on his great designs in bringing
such a race of men to people the shores of this great continent!
What other people on earth can point to such an ancestry as the
people of New England? . . . Under every earthly disadvan-
tage, with incredible toil, in the midst of appalling dangers,
obstructed by the jealousy of the mother country, and at last
compelled to counter her in arms, in two centuries the people, rich in nothing save the principles of the Pilgrims, have
turned this wilderness into a fruitful field; and made it the
moral garden of the whole world.*

Of course, nothing does more for a fledgling publishing house
than its first bestseller. I might not be writing this account today
were it not for the big sale, at the very beginning of our history,
of a two-volume work titled *Napoleon and His Marshals* by the
Reverend (surprised?) J. T. Headley. By all accounts it was far
from being the model of historical accuracy—but then, how many
bestsellers are? More to the point, it satisfied a widespread interest
among Americans in Napoleon a generation after his death. It
was common in those days for businessmen to display a bust of
Napoleon in their offices. He had his cult revival; Charles had the
book. By 1861 it had gone through fifty printings. He also had as
a result of his marriage to Emma Elizabeth Blair in 1848—two
years after the firm was founded—what historian John Delaney
described as "failure insurance." Her father, the railroad tycoon
John Insley Blair, was at the time one of the richest men in America. He was eventually to own more miles of railroad track than
anyone in the world, and more acres of land—over a million—
than any other American, including even his more famous contemporary competitor Commodore Vanderbilt. He was devoted
to his son-in-law, who addressed him as Father in their many
letters preserved at Princeton, where Blair was an eventual trustee
and benefactor.

Among the letters between Charles and his father-in-law is one in which the former prays for a deeper Christian faith beyond the latter's nominal adherence to his Scottish Presbyterian roots. I had for many years a small Blair treasure handed down the line: the eighteen-year-old John I. Blair's 1820 hymnal of handwritten transcriptions of lyrics and musical notations in his crisp sepia calligraphy. I gave it a decade ago to my son Charles when his first daughter, Elizabeth Blair, was christened. Blair was clearly raised in the faith. Those later devout lines of beseeching and preaching from his young son-in-law—a risky if pious epistle—seem to have been taken not amiss but to heart. By the end of his life, the railroad billionaire had built and donated one hundred Presbyterian churches across the country; he named Scribner, Nebraska, in honor of Charles. My brother Blair has driven out to visit it twice (along with the larger Blair, Nebraska). On his first trip, he was interviewed by the local newspaper. "Because your name is Blair Scribner?" I queried. "No," he replied. "Because they said I was the only New Yorker ever to have done so." Shortly before the paterfamilias died at the ripe age of ninety-seven (he outlived his son-in-law by twenty-eight years and his daughter Emma by thirty), his grandson Ledyard Blair began constructing a massive Neo-Renaissance mansion called Blairsden, looming like the House of Usher over an artificial lake—Blair Lake, what else?—in Peapack, New Jersey. We all swam in that lake as children; the mansion had by then become a convent. The elder, frugal Blair was asked by a friend why he had always lived in the same farmhouse all his life while his grandson was planning a chateau. He replied that there was a huge difference between Ledyard and himself. "You see, he has a rich grandfather—and I don't."

But back to the books. Between bestsellers there were the more familiar and trying cases where the first book or, worse, books by an author proved disappointing. For instance, there was Donald G. Mitchell, who wrote under the pen name "Ik Marvel" and came to Scribner after a non-best-selling debut at another house.

Charles decided to invest in Mitchell's future and published his second book, *Battle Summer*, about the author's travels in Europe during the revolutions of 1848. It was equally underwhelming in sales. But his next book, published the following year, *Reveries of a Bachelor*, took off at once and the long hoped-for-success was won in spades. (I think the title may have helped.) From then on, Ik Marvel was, as we say in the trade, a "name author"—if a name long since forgotten. Curiously enough, a century later while my father was clearing out for sale the Scribner printing plant and warehouse on West Forty-Third Street in New York City, he came upon the original lead printing plates for *Reveries of a Bachelor*. No one could explain why for so many decades they had escaped the fate of being melted down for a new book. Perhaps through a series of oversights, but perhaps equally as a result of the irrational respect publishers retain for a bestseller—even the past century's.

In 1850, Isaac Baker died, which left Charles alone. He bought out Baker's share and renamed the firm "Charles Scribner & Company." It was a period of growth, and there were several new projects in the pipeline that put the new house on the map. That house soon began its own northward trek up the map of the city. In 1856, owing to the announced sale of the Brick Church property, it moved to 377–379 Broadway; two years later it moved to the Brooks Building at 124 Grand Street off Broadway. The year before, Charles had taken on as a minority partner another Charles—Charles Welford, son of a London bookseller—to start an importing business of English books, called Scribner & Welford. Within a decade, in 1864, Welford moved to London and the American publishing house established a presence there that lasted until my college days.

During those early years Charles had been building a fine list of books on religion. This program reached a high point around the time of the Civil War when he set out to publish an American version of the towering work of biblical scholarship by German Calvinist theologian Johann Peter Lange, his *Biblical Commentary*.

Those lean years during the war might have challenged not only such an ambitious project but indeed the very survival of the house were it not for the godsend of Blair as a father-in-law who provided key loans at critical moments—all of which, I must stress, his son-in-law repaid as religiously as promptly. Eventually completed by 1880 in twenty-five large volumes—financed at an enormous cost by Charles Scribner (and later his sons)—the set was both a commercial and a critical success. It was copublished in Great Britain by Clark of Edinburgh—something of a feather in the cap of our American firm since Clark had already begun his own translation of Lange, which he then dropped in favor of the Scribner edition. Publishing ties are often old and binding, and here we have a good case in point since almost a hundred years later the houses of Scribner and T & T Clark once again collaborated on a revision of the *Hastings' Dictionary of the Bible*, published by my dad in 1963 when I was a schoolboy and still selling strong when I joined the firm a dozen years later.

In 1865 Charles Scribner & Company took its first step into magazine publishing with the somewhat staid—that's an understatement—*Hours at Home: A Popular Magazine of Religious and Useful Literature*. It was presented as a publication that would bring into every home the virtues by which Americans were supposed to live. Today it would be dubbed a "family values" magazine. The first issue included, among other gems, two short biographies of early Christian saints, an article on the rivers of Palestine, and in a similar vein an account of the unsuccessful attempt by missionaries to get the king of the Hawaiian islands to give up drinking. The magazine—unlike the missionaries—was successful, and plans were soon afoot to transform it into something far more ambitious. Two years later it was followed by another Scribner journal, *The Book Buyer: A Summary of American and Foreign Literature*. It would be Scribner's longest-running magazine until it folded in 1938.

By this time Scribner had taken on a new partner, Andrew Armstrong, and together they moved the firm in 1866 still farther uptown, to 654 Broadway, where they would remain for the next eight years. The next year they were joined by *New York Times* journalist and editor Edward Seymour, and in 1869 the eldest of Charles's three sons, John Blair, left Princeton early, three months before his nineteenth birthday, to join his father at the house. His mother had died the month before, at the age of forty-one, just five days after giving birth to her youngest child, Isabelle.

In 1870 a new and separate firm, Scribner & Company, was formed to publish that more ambitious successor to *Hours at Home*, an "illustrated magazine for the people" called *Scribner's Monthly*. The key players, in addition to the original Scribner partners, were Scribner novelist and poet Josiah Gilbert Holland—who wrote under the pen name Timothy Titcomb—and Roswell Smith. They had met in Europe and decided to team up to produce a magazine of American literature and art—with a decided emphasis on *American*. Charles Scribner had made a similar proposal to Holland before he set sail. By the time he returned with Smith, it had grown into something too grand—and independent—to be housed within the book company. Scribner agreed to lend his name to it as a minority partner. Holland was the editor; Smith the business manager. It was a roaring success from the start. A hundred years later, in 1971, my father collected the first twelve issues of *Scribner's Monthly* and had them published in a single massive volume to celebrate the 125th anniversary of the family publishing house. I still have my copy. A decade ago, art historian Page Knox wrote her doctoral dissertation on our family magazine, which Columbia describes in its catalog entry as "arguably the most prominent monthly magazine during the 1870s. Initiating improvements in reproduction technology and art criticism, Scribner played a major role in the development of the nation's art world in the Gilded Age, transforming the reception, perception, and consumption of images by the American public."

Sadly, the founding Charles did not live to see its success, for he died of typhoid fever that summer in Lucerne, Switzerland. He had gone abroad in the hope of improving his poor health. Before leaving, he wrote a new last will, which sadly proved to be just that. I came upon a copy of it at Princeton a few months ago, and its opening passage struck me as both poignant and true to character: "In the name of God, Amen. I, Charles Scribner of the City of New York, Publisher, being of sound and disposing mind but mindful of the uncertainty of life do make and declare this to be my last Will and Testament." He was fifty years old. His eldest son, John Blair, who was to take over the company, had just turned twenty-one. Charles was temporarily buried beside his late wife in the family vault of the Marble Cemetery in the East Village, close to his childhood home, before they were moved to the new family plot he had recently purchased at Woodlawn Cemetery in the Bronx, our final destination ever since. Their headstones are inscribed "Father" and "Mother." The firm was now in the hands of a young bachelor, who would take the reins for the next seven and a half years and prove a worthy namesake of his grandfather Blair.

Chapter 2

Sons and Successors

When the founding Charles died, he left behind not only his eldest son to run the firm but also four younger children, who were now orphans ranging in age from two to nineteen: two sons, Charles and Arthur, and two daughters, Emma and Isabelle. (His two other children, Herbert and Annie, had died in infancy. Their diminutive graves are also in the plot at Woodlawn, a reminder of how vulnerable young children were to illness in the late 1800s.) The weight placed on the sole legal adult in the household, John Blair, must have been daunting. His sixty-nine-year-old grandfather and namesake became his chief source of emotional as well as financial support. A letter from John Blair to his younger brother Charles reveals a renewed bond of affection and mutual support that would soon turn into a professional partnership. But that remained four years in the future. Charles was only seventeen and about to enter Princeton, which he—unlike his older brother—would enjoy for a full four years until his graduation in 1875. Youngest brother Arthur was only twelve at the time of his father's death, so his joining the house of writers lay still farther in the future—and beyond the lifetime of his eldest brother (spoiler alert). The three sons were to work in pairs, but sadly never all together.

Yet this was hardly a period of marking time. The next year, 1872, John Blair formed two new partnerships: the first with Andrew Armstrong and Edward Seymour for the ongoing book company now called "Scribner, Armstrong & Company," and the second with Charles Welford and Armstrong to run a book importing company for the next six years. Then in 1873 a separate magazine partnership, Scribner & Company, launched a new periodical, *St. Nicholas: Scribner's Illustrated Magazine for Girls and Boys*. Its editor, Mary Mapes Dodge, became famous in her own right that same month of November when her first book was published by Scribner: *Hans Brinker; or, The Silver Skates*—a book that holds a special place in my heart and childhood memory since it was first read to me by my mother, a lifelong and professional figure skater. I still have the copy on my shelf.

In December of 1874 the three book partners Scribner, Armstrong, and Seymour decided to move to larger quarters still farther up Broadway, 743–745 (between Astor Place and Eighth Street). Today apartment buildings rise over the site of both houses. It was to be their publishing home for the next nineteen years. Six months later, after his Princeton graduation, the second Charles joined Blair at the firm. Over the next few years several key events shaped the house's future and turned it into a purely *family* business, which it would remain for over a century.

In 1877 Seymour died and his shares were purchased by the two remaining partners. A year later Armstrong retired to set up his own firm (long since forgotten) and his shares were purchased by Scribner. The book publishing house (as distinct from the magazine) was at last fully in family hands and its name changed to "Charles Scribner's Sons," a fitting monument to the founder. The importing company was now simply "Scribner & Welford," with Charles Welford overseeing the acquisition of foreign books for New York. But the banner event of that year was the coming of age of the subscription book department. It had been established six years earlier to sell Henry M. Stanley's first—and instantly famous—Scribner book, *How I Found Livingstone: Travels, Adventures, and Discoveries in Central Africa, Including Four Months Residence with Dr. Livingstone.* In association with Messrs. Black of Edinburgh, Scribners (shorthand for Charles Scribner's Sons) brought out the first American edition (the ninth edition) of the *Encyclopedia Britannica* and sold some seventy thousand sets—four times as many as sold in Britain! In those days publishers liked to play up sales figures with various imaginary calculations. Scribners advertised that all those volumes laid end to end would reach "from New York to beyond Omaha"—an inspiring image! It gives new credence to Scribner, Nebraska.

In later years the subscription department published library sets of the works of such famous authors as Kipling, Stevenson, Henry James, and J. M. Barrie, to name just a few. At the other end of the scale was the Scribner Music Library, a multivolume set of piano music, which I kept on top of my upright to inspire me during all those hours of childhood practice. Its successor, the Scribner reference book department, was to become a century later the premier publisher of reference works such as the *Dictionary of American Biography*, the *Dictionary of American History*, the *Dictionary of Scientific Biography*, the *Dictionary of the History of Ideas*, and the *Dictionary of the Middle Ages* and all the periods before and after—redundancy in excellence is no sin. No surprise my father considered it his crown jewel. But that's for a later chapter.

Back to 1878, *Britannica*, Blair, and Charles. The dawn of so much promise for the brothers was soon eclipsed by tragedy a year later when at twenty-eight John Blair, by all family accounts, worked himself to death. He had been married to Lucy Skidmore Scribner for less than four years when shortly before Christmas he fell ill, but he was soon found back at his desk. Then in January of 1879 he suffered a second attack of pneumonia, which at first was not considered life-threatening. A few days later his brother stopped by after work to visit him, and according to the report in the *New York Times*, "They conversed on the topics of the day." Yet Charles "could not refrain from confessing his fears that the illness of his brother might be dangerous, when the elder brother arose in his bed and playfully said, 'Cheer up, old fellow; you always look on the dark side; I shall soon be all right again.' Then, throwing up his arms, he gave one long sigh and expired." Attending that final scene worthy of Verdi's *Traviata* were just Charles, Lucy, and two physicians.

Blair left Lucy a childless widow of twenty-five. She never remarried. Eighteen years later, in 1897, she moved to Saratoga and bought a house along with four adjacent lots, where in 1903 she established the Young Women's Industrial Club, which in 1911 became the Skidmore School of Arts and finally Skidmore College in 1922. She became the college's chief benefactor until her death in 1931—thanks largely to her inheritance from John Blair—and her original home, Scribner House, eventually became the residence of Skidmore's president. The college library is aptly named Scribner Library. Her brother-in-law Charles was a trustee of the college, followed by his son Charles, her nephew, and finally by my father. My sole connection is more oblique. Two decades ago I was asked to write a recommendation to Skidmore for a classmate of my son Charlie. I had never written a successful one. This time I decided to include a photograph of Lucy's grave in our family plot and noted—truthfully, just a few years after my dad's death—that I visited it each year. He got in.

CHAPTER 3

Charles in Charge

AT TWENTY-FIVE, CHARLES SCRIBNER II FOUND HIMSELF ALONE at the helm of Charles Scribner's Sons. From the start, he was to have his hands full. But he embodied what would become his grandson's, my father's, mantra: "No rush, just do it immediately." Two months after Blair's sudden death, CS II hired Edward L. Burlingame, son of the American minister to China and a gifted editor and journalist in his own right, as the company's literary adviser. It was an inspired hire, as would become clear before the end of his first decade at the firm. Scribner renewed the partnership with Welford in London, which would prove to be equally fortuitous by the roster of preeminent British authors soon to be published by the firm in New York.

On a less promising note, there were rumblings in the magazine subsidiary, Scribner & Company. The nonfamily majority owners, it seemed, chafed at being in any way beholden to Charles Scribner's Sons—perhaps they chafed at being beholden to a twenty-five-year-old. They soon talked of publishing books themselves; each side regarded the other as the tail trying to wag the dog. When one of the outside partners, Roswell Smith, bought up enough shares to acquire individual control of the company in 1881, the delicate balance was disturbed, to put it mildly. Scribner refused to retain a minority interest in a publishing company that bore his name. He sold his share of the magazine company to Smith and the other partners. Thus the celebrated *Scribner's Monthly* and *St. Nicholas Magazine* passed forever out of the hands of the Scribner family. It was a clean break. Under the terms of the agreement the company was to be reincorporated under a new name: the Century Company. *Scribner's Monthly* was renamed the *Century Magazine* and the rest, as they say, is history. More telling—indeed prophetic—was the requirement in return that Charles Scribner agree to stay out of the magazine business for five years. Judging from what happens later, it is clear that the buyers had good reason for this moratorium; Charles would keep his eye on the clock.

The next decisive step taken by CS II involved Scribners' textbook business. Beginning in the 1850s the firm had built up a solid and celebrated list of schoolbooks. But this area of publishing was becoming increasingly specialized, perhaps too much so for a young publisher who preferred to focus on popular, literary, and scholarly books ranging from the thirteen-volume series *Campaigns of the Civil War*—the first two of which appeared in 1881—to *What to Do and How to Do It: The American Boys Handy Book*, published the following year. Its author, the truly immortal Dan Beard, would become a founder of the Boy Scouts of America. Truly immortal? Well, this artist and naturalist was born in 1850, and when I joined the firm in 1975 and took over our paperback line a year later we were still getting letters addressed to him. More telling of my cluelessness was that when I was told to add, as a new paperback on the list, the steadily selling title *Shelters, Shacks, and Shanties* by D. C. Beard, I tried (very hard) to locate its countercultural, "back-to-nature" author before discovering that he had been dead for thirty-five years and that the book had originally been published by my great-grandfather in 1910! But back to the textbooks. My young great-grandfather, CS II, announced in 1883 the sale of his entire list of school books to Ivison, Blakeman, Taylor & Company, then one of the largest educational publishers in the United States. Within four years of taking over, solo, he had pruned the firm down. But his pruning, as every arborist knows, had a positive purpose.

Scribner was by nature a builder. We can be sure that while part of the business was being dismantled he had already begun to think about something bigger and better to set up in its place. The new educational department that he started a decade after the sale of the old one is a case in point.

On the home front, life soon brightened for Charles. In 1882 he married the lovely Louise Flagg, daughter of Episcopal clergyman and portrait painter Jared Flagg from Hartford. Three of her brothers were noted painters: Montague Flagg, George Whiting Flagg, and more famously Charles Noël Flagg, whose portrait of the family's Hartford friend and neighbor Mark Twain hangs today in the Metropolitan Museum. (I have his painting of Tom Sawyer, a family heirloom I treasure.) Their great-uncle was the American Romantic painter Washington Allston, whose youthful portrait my mother and I gave to the Princeton Art Museum in 2005 in memory of my father and in honor of our most recent graduate named Charles. Montague painted a portrait of his young brother-in-law Charles, now hanging at the Princeton University Press, and a posthumous one of the founding Charles, which hung for three generations in my father's old office on Fifth Avenue before we moved out and I took it home. The most famous of the siblings, the architect Ernest Flagg, would soon become the firm's and family's architect of choice. Nepotism was also a family business.

The year before, 1881, Charles's younger brother, Arthur Hawley Scribner, having graduated from Princeton, came into the firm to help him. (This is a familiar refrain, literally, and will recur at regular intervals throughout our history.) That same year also saw the publication of artist, illustrator, and pioneer of comics A. B. Frost's first of many books, *Stuff and Nonsense*. Frost and his publisher would later become good friends and neighbors in New

Jersey. The two Scribner brothers formed a fruitful partnership that lasted almost half a century before their deaths two years apart. Always in Charles's shadow—surely by fraternal design—Arthur's natural social gifts made him the perfect complement to his demanding and serious—some would say imperious—elder brother. In 1879 he was a founding member of the Ivy Club, the first of the eating clubs at Princeton, and was later elected its first president. His portrait still hangs over the grand staircase. I felt most at home in that secular social chapel as an undergraduate—and still do a half century later. His Princeton class was to elect him "president for life." His domain—and expertise—at Scribners was the physical production of every book, from design to printing and binding, promotion, and distribution. But he was also the link between the house and local charities, and his own qualities of charity and modesty made him the go-to intercessor for Scribner staff to approach in lieu of Charles Scribner II himself. It all worked well, though I cannot—with two younger brothers of my own—help wonder about the personal price he paid for playing the supporting role so gamely.

Scribners soon benefited from Charles's initial pruning; the remaining branches flowered as never before. Many of the American authors the firm introduced are still revered. George Washington Cable first appeared in print in *Scribner's Monthly* in 1873 with the short story "Sieur George." Six years later several of his stories were collected and published as the beloved *Old Creole Days*. Another cherished Southern voice was Thomas Nelson Page, whose book *In Ole Virginia* was the first of his many about the South.

Now lest it be thought our firm was the literary heir to the Confederacy alone, I hasten to add some authors from up north, closer to home. There was the illustrious Henry Adams (the most New England of names). His *History of the United States* was published in 1889 in nine volumes, and his ironic letters to his publisher offer a standard for any difficult author to follow.

Henry Van Dyke, "poet, preacher, university teacher, diplomat" (to quote our *Dictionary of American Biography*) and described by a Princeton colleague as the only man "able to strut while sitting down," started out on the Scribner list in 1888 with a pamphlet titled *The National Sin of Literary Piracy*. How that must have warmed his publisher's heart! A few years later the prolific author wrote another book that caused an awkward hiccup in our history. That book was titled *Fisherman's Luck*, and to the publisher's bad luck, the title appeared with a prominent and most regrettable single-letter misprint that almost instantly put Scribners out of business and the author into an early grave.

On a brighter note, the decade witnessed the appearance of famous children's books on the list: Howard Pyle's *The Merry Adventures of Robin Hood* in 1883 and Frances Hodgson Burnett's *Little Lord Fauntleroy* in 1886. The previous year saw the debut of Robert Louis Stevenson on the Scribner roster with *A Child's Garden of Verses*. A later edition of this classic with illustrations by Jesse Wilcox Smith was one of the original titles in the "Scribner Illustrated Classics," still in print today and renowned for their magnificent illustrations by Howard Pyle, Maxfield Parrish, N. C. Wyeth, and other notable painters of the Brandywine School. Stevenson would follow the next year, 1886, with his *Strange Case of Dr. Jekyll and Mr. Hyde* and then *Kidnapped*, one of the year's bestsellers.

Stevenson was to become not only one of the firm's most prolific authors—alongside Rudyard Kipling and Henry James—but the most loyal of all. My dad's candidate for that honor would later be Hemingway, but I'd give the trophy to Stevenson thanks to the discovery in the 1980s by Princeton curator John Delaney of an unpublished Stevenson letter hiding in plain sight in our archives. In 1887 Stevenson was outraged by Harper's publishing a pirated edition of his books (taking advantage of the lack of international copyright protection that Van Dyke above bemoaned). Admitting their deed, which deprived the author of his American royalties, they sent him a check for a paltry twenty pounds. Stevenson decried this crass behavior and published his protest in the press. When the author came to America he stayed with his good friend Charles Fairchild, who was enlisted by Harper's to repair relations with the hope of luring Stevenson to their house. Stevenson would have none of it, as his response to Fairchild made clear in a personal letter that was finally shared with Scribners some thirty-three years later by Fairchild's widow after all the players were no longer living. I first read the letter in Delaney's article for our 1996 sesquicentennial shortly after my father's death, and the key passage of Stevenson's missive brought tears to my eyes—and still does:

> *I am very sure you act entirely as my friend, in this matter; and I thank you sincerely for the trouble you have been at, and I give you my kind expressions. Frankly, nothing would induce me to leave the Scribners; they came forward and used me thoroughly well when no one else did; I believe they find a profit in me; and there is no nameable amount of dollars that would make me pay them back evil for good.*

Today authors change publishers as casually as they change accountants. That was another era—and author. Noting that Scribners would go on to publish most of Stevenson's books during his lifetime and five separate posthumous editions of his entire opus—the last, in 1925, comprising thirty-two volumes—Delaney concluded, "Clearly Stevenson's loyalty was repaid."

During the 1880s Charles II was mulling ideas for a new magazine as he waited out the mandatory five-year moratorium. It was virtually inconceivable that he could have been content without a magazine. As a lad of fifteen he had started up a little comic monthly called *Merry Moments* and soon had to give it up, not because it proved unsuccessful, but because to his father's way of thinking it was far *too* successful for a full-time schoolboy. Few were surprised, then, in December of 1886 when the clock struck twelve, so to speak, and the firm announced the new *Scribner's Magazine*. Charles held the first annual Scribner's Magazine Dinner at his townhouse on Thirty-Eighth Street. The Christmas spirits must have been soaring. Its original editor, from 1887 to 1914, was Edward Burlingame, who had been Scribner's literary adviser since 1879. His editorial talents would now be given full rein as he began to turn the new magazine into something finer and more successful than even its ambitious thirty-two-year-old founder would have dared to foresee.

To tell the story of *Scribner's Magazine*, to do justice to its multifaceted contributions to American literature, art, and life for more than half a century, is beyond the scope of my story. In addition to the art contained in all those monthly issues—the advertising posters themselves are valuable collectibles today—its history includes those very writers whose books helped build the reputation of the publishing firm over the ensuing decades of literary preeminence. The magazine was, in effect, a double asset to Charles Scribner's Sons, not only in itself as a profitable publication—its first issue selling an impressive 140,000 copies—but also as a golden net for new talent who would follow with many successful books for Scribners. Edith Wharton, for one, launched her literary career with her 1890 story "Mrs. Manstey's View" in *Scribner's Magazine*. Across the Atlantic it would haul in and feature (along with Stevenson) such stellar British talents as James M. Barrie, Rudyard Kipling, and John Galsworthy.

In January of 1890, a new Charles appeared on the scene—or rather, in the nursery: my grandfather, Charles Scribner III. Scribners now had a son and heir to keep the firm's plural title intact. But his story must await the next century. In June of that year the firm published Stanley's *In Darkest Africa*. In view of baby Charles III's future wife's (my grandmother's) late penchant for African photo safaris—she took fourteen as a widow in her seventies and eighties—and his granddaughter's marriage to the safari guide and her move to Kenya, I'm tempted to make a connection, but I'll resist. The next year, Scribner & Welford was merged into the New York firm as the London branch of Charles Scribner's Sons. More important from a publishing perspective, CS II finally succeeded in remedying the "national sin" of piracy by playing a key role on the Joint Committee of the American Copyright League and getting Congress to pass the first International Copyright Bill. Stevenson surely smiled with approval.

In May 1894, the firm capped fifteen years under CS II by moving north into a stately, six-story building on Fifth Avenue and Twenty-First Street designed by the renowned Beaux-Arts architect Ernest Flagg. This commission, by his brother-in-law, would mark the first of many celebrated buildings—and future landmarks—by Flagg, who got his start in the profession by sketching ideas for renovations to his cousins Alice and Cornelius Vanderbilt II's huge mansion on Fifth Avenue and Fifty-Eighth Street (the site of Bergdorf Goodman today, next to the Plaza). It was the largest private mansion ever built in New York, and the Vanderbilts, impressed by Flagg's gifts, paid for his education at the École des Beaux-Arts in Paris from 1889 to 1891. He designed the new building for Scribners within two years of his return—sometimes nepotism pays dividends to both sides. The building was the first in the country to house, behind its classical façade, all the chief activities of publishing (save printing). The ground floor featured a magnificent bookstore, the prototype for the later, larger, and more famous one on Forty-Eighth and Fifth.

A contemporary magazine description notes: "Instead of a confused and crowded space with counters and low bookcases, the whole room resembles a particularly well-cared-for library in some great private house." The second floor housed the editorial and business offices, then the magazine floor, then the subscription department floor, then warehousing, and finally mailing, shipping, and miscellanea on the sixth and top floor. Clearly there was an implied hierarchy of convenience; the boss and his editors worked on the *piano nobile*, one flight up from the street. Flagg's future monuments, in addition to those for his Scribner relations, were to include the main buildings in Annapolis, St. Luke's Hospital, the Corcoran Gallery (Washington, DC), Pomfret School, Sheldon Library at St. Paul's School (New Hampshire), and in lower Manhattan the Singer Tower, which for one brief shining moment rose higher than any building in the world. By the last decade of the nineteenth century the Gilded Age was at high noon and Scribners was enjoying its own Golden Age as the premier publisher of American literature.

In 1896, Scribners celebrated its golden (fiftieth) anniversary at its fifth annual Christmas Dinner at the St. Denis Hotel in New York. Those temporal dinners left mementos worthy of collection and publication as art books. The menu for the next year's dinner, according to *Publishers Weekly*, "was an artistic booklet bound in parchment paper covers" designed and illustrated by the great Maxfield Parrish, whose paintings today sell for millions of dollars. "The contents were in imitation of an alphabet book, beginning with 'H is for *huîtres—céleri, canapés divers, olives* . . . and V is for *vin*,' with the significant hint, 'please pay at the desk.'"

But that golden anniversary shone all the brighter by a roster of stellar bestsellers: Frances Hodgson Burnett's *A Lady of Quality* and J. M. Barrie's *Sentimental Tommie*, followed by his *Margaret Ogilvy*. Of course Barrie is remembered today primarily for *Peter Pan*, but he would have to await the next century to take off. On a loftier plane, a young philosophy professor at Harvard, George Santayana, debuted that year with his book on aesthetics, *The Sense of Beauty*. Four decades later, in 1935, his best-selling novel *The Last Puritan* would be published by Scribners. I cannot think of another philosopher equally versatile in letters. (His more famous students included T. S. Eliot, Justice Felix Frankfurter, Robert Frost, and Gertrude Stein—quite a legacy.) Still in the pipeline were books that would add equal luster to the following year, 1897: the first volume (of thirty-six!) of Rudyard Kipling's works—the "Outward Bound Edition"—which would take another forty years to complete. There were advantages to being a family company. Can anyone imagine a public corporation today undertaking a work requiring such patience and perseverance?

The end of this banner year brought forth a book of pictures brighter than words: *London as Seen by Charles Dana Gibson*, the creator of the iconic "Gibson Girl." He would have a long and fruitful association with the house. But the year closed with a most unusual debut by one of our greatest novelists of all time, a worthy match for Fitzgerald and Hemingway in the following century: Edith Wharton. Why unusual? Because it was a book titled *The Decoration of Houses*, coauthored by Ogden Codman Jr. Wharton had a keen eye for architecture and gardens—she wrote several brilliant books on both—but she is not remembered primarily for her decorating. Yet that debut is still available in several editions today.

I must not, alas, leave 1897 without acknowledging a loss. Its magnitude would not be evident for many years to come, but in hindsight it was major. Not just because he was the business manager of the magazine or because he had come to Scribners twenty years earlier as a fourteen-year-old lad carrying books from the bindery to the packing room. No, it is because his name was Frank Nelson Doubleday. He felt called to a greater role in publishing, and he fulfilled it. He founded his own publishing house, which would eventually grow into a dominant American company the next century, the last to own its own presses, before his grandson sold it to buy a baseball team, the New York Mets. If only my great-grandfather had made Doubleday a partner. But that's history—and with a nice twist. My first memoir and spiritual journal, *The Shadow of God*, was published by Doubleday in 2006 because my editor of choice, Michelle Rapkin, happened to be the new publisher of Doubleday's religious books division. As Albert Einstein observed, "Coincidences are God's way of remaining anonymous."

But I must not leave that decade on a downbeat. Fortunately a future US president may claim credit for closing this chapter—and century—on a note of glory: Theodore Roosevelt. His first book, *The Rough Riders*, appeared on the Scribner list in May 1899, marking the beginning of a long and illustrious career, in and out of office, between the covers of many books. The Scribner staff understandably went a bit overboard when the author moved to the White House. On one book jacket the copywriter hailed Roosevelt as the "American Homer," which elicited a spate of scornful letters from readers protesting the hyperbole. The embarrassed president asked his editor, "Why couldn't you have said *Herodotus?*"

CHAPTER 4

Books and Bricks

THE NEW CENTURY DAWNING IN 1900 HAS BEEN DUBBED "THE American Century." The American Publishers Association was organized with Charles Scribner II as its first president. Admittedly its original purpose—to regulate the price of copyrighted books in America—was later deemed unconstitutional as price-fixing under the Sherman Anti-Trust Act, but the idea of such a professional association took root. Six decades later Scribner's grandson, my father, would serve as president of the American Book Publishers Council, a successor organization founded after the Second World War and the precursor of today's Association of American Publishers. The next year witnessed the range of Scribner's literary vision: from the Russian Marxist revolutionary Maxim Gorky to the stately Henry James, who appeared on the list with *The Sacred Fount*. Sadly, James's greatest fame was to come long after his death, but he did live to see Scribners publish the great "New York Edition"—twenty-four volumes in all—in 1910, which my father reissued in its entirety in the 1950s.

James is a difficult author to read—beyond my patience—but of towering importance to the history of literature. I confess that my enjoyment of his works has been based on their translations to glorious films—from *The Innocents* (his haunting novella *The Turn of the Screw*) to *The Europeans*, *The Bostonians*, *The Heiress*

(*Washington Square*), *The Portrait of a Lady, The Golden Bowl, Daisy Miller*, and *The Wings of the Dove*. They are all worth watching—perhaps even reading. The next year witnessed his good friend Edith Wharton's novel debut: *The Valley of Decision*, an ambitious two-volume historical saga set in northern Italy during the years of the French Revolution. It was followed three years later by her more memorable achievement, *The House of Mirth*, which hit the bestseller lists for two years.

In 1902, the Scribner brothers—I say brothers plural since Arthur was surely a prime mover—opened their own printing plant on Pearl Street (spurred on by the demanding success of the magazine) and had Maxfield Parrish design for it the most elegant colophon since the Renaissance. Three years later, in 1905, they purchased a large lot on West Forty-Third Street on which to build a new printing plant and warehouse. The architect was, once again, Charles's brother-in-law Ernest Flagg, who a year before had renovated Arthur's townhouse on East Sixty-Seventh Street with the grandest Beaux-Arts limestone façade on the block. Perhaps inspired—or not to be outdone—by his younger brother, who had the family eye for art and design, Charles would commission from scratch his own Flagg townhouse of Belgian brick a couple of blocks away, on East Sixty-Sixth Street, where my father often stayed as a child whenever his parents were away. It featured an interior entrance for autos that were taken down to the basement in an elevator, then rotated on a turntable before rising and departing out the wrought-iron gate. Flagg was as inventive as stylish. His new red-brick printing plant was an inspired mix of industrial restraint and discreet classical flourishes. Six decades after my father closed the press and sold the building in the 1950s, it has been recently renovated for state-of-the-art office condos. The two townhouses also remain standing, awaiting similar renovation and resale. I've toured them both, but I'm not about to take the bait. As F. Scott Fitzgerald wrote, "The victor belongs to the spoils."

Between construction and moving into the new printing plant, CS II undertook two major projects. The first, in 1906, was publishing the initial twenty-three volumes of the Elkhorn Edition of *The Works of Theodore Roosevelt.* He was then President Roosevelt and a regular correspondent with his publisher, whom the Rough Rider used as his eyes and ears in the New York business community. Scribner was a fond fan of Roosevelt, though at times was put off by the president's towering ego. The publisher, who once circled every capital "I" on an office memo, was equally dismayed by Roosevelt's excessive use of what he called "the vertical pronoun." In fact, the Scribner plant had to send out for hundreds more of them to be cast in lead in order to typeset Roosevelt's latest book.

Closer to home, CS II donated for the benefit of his alma mater the Princeton University Press, incorporated in 1906 with Scribner as its first president. It had been founded the year before as the "Princeton Alumni Press" by a young alumnus, Whitney Darrow, with Scribner's support, in a rented office above a drugstore on Nassau Street to print the alumni magazine. Scribner had a grander vision: He wanted to establish and endow for the university a full-fledged scholarly publishing house. Together with Darrow he forged ahead. Hiring once again his brother-in-law, Scribner sent Flagg a postcard from Antwerp of its famous Plantin Press (for which Rubens designed title pages). He wanted Princeton University Press to have an inviting courtyard and publishing presence in town equal to that of the Plantin's abroad. Flagg did not disappoint. Today the press boasts the loveliest of the Princeton courts, recently replanted as a little Eden, complete with central tree. The building was eventually named in honor of its donor. A half century later, my dad served as its president and trustee, like his father and grandfather before him. Succeeding him as a young trustee, I always enjoyed those visits across the Hudson to my favorite publishing house in the country. In 2005, I attended its centennial festivities with our son Charlie, a few weeks before his Princeton graduation—the fifth of his name to participate in celebrating that premier press.

Back in New York a century earlier, the year concluded on a high note indeed: the December 1906 publication of J. M. Barrie's *Peter Pan in Kensington Gardens*, the first American edition of this children's classic about the airborne boy who wouldn't grow up. In my youth before I could read, it was translated into a Broadway musical starring Mary Martin flying high above the stage on a wire, a year after Disney launched Peter Pan onto the cinema screen with glorious animations. I remember better the television film with Martin in 1960, by which time I could read the book. From the age of three, our younger son, Christopher, was obsessed with Captain Hook, whom he impersonated three decades before becoming himself a captain in the US Army.

That book would be followed on our list within two years by an equally famous classic, *The Wind in the Willows*, by Kenneth Grahame, to be illustrated by a series of artists—most notably Arthur Rackham and Ernest Shepherd—for Scribner editions. But we almost missed publishing it. My great-grandfather was against it; he considered it a silly book that "only a child would enjoy." But fortunately he was overruled—by none other than President Roosevelt, who told him he was wrong, he must publish it, it was a classic. That was surely the most enduring contribution from the White House to our house.

By that time, my teenage grandfather Charles Scribner III was up north at St. Paul's School in New Hampshire studying in the new Sheldon Library, designed by his Uncle Ernest. Surely Charles's devout Episcopalian mother must get the credit for the choice of so remote—if distinguished—a school for their only son, as she gently but firmly replanted the Scribner family in her church. She would later have her brother design a garden chapel at "The Gables" in Morristown, New Jersey, for which she compiled—and her husband obligingly printed—an exquisite leather-bound prayerbook titled *Light of Life, a Book of Prayer for Use in the Chapel of St. Mary of the Angels*. It never made the bestseller list, but the Scribner religion list would thereafter lean more heavily toward Anglican (and even include Catholic) publications, as the firm was to be led by the next two generations of confirmed Episcopalians. (That must have sent our Puritan forebears spinning.)

The autumn my grandfather followed his two namesakes to Princeton saw the publication of the first of former president Roosevelt's African hunting articles. It marked the highest circulation ever attained by *Scribner's Magazine* to date—in fact, the highest ever reached by any high-priced American magazine. I hung the original artwork for its cover, a magnificent (and politically apt) elephant, in our younger son's room long before discovering its significance. That magazine splash was followed the next year, 1910, by Roosevelt's book *African Game Trails*, and the following year by three banner classics—Edith Wharton's *Ethan Frome*, J. M. Barrie's *Peter Pan and Wendy* (which, illustrated, introduced Neverland and Captain Hook to generations of children), and the first of the new Scribner Illustrated Classics series: Stevenson's *Treasure Island*, illustrated with specially commissioned oil paintings by N. C. Wyeth. I recall seeing several of them on the walls of our publishing offices until the early 1970s when they were sold and donated to the Brandywine Museum. When my father reissued this classic to mark its centennial in 1981—the year his namesake grandson was born—he had all the Wyeth paintings rephotographed and printed with far higher resolution than those in the original edition. He received a glowing handwritten letter of thanks and praise from the artist's even more famous son, Andrew Wyeth, who wrote a similar one to me after we continued those reissues with Stevenson's (and Wyeth's) *Kidnapped*. I treasure those letters even more today since the curator at the Brandywine Museum recently told me that Wyeth rarely wrote such letters, and she asked me to send her photocopies.

In 1912, Charles II purchased a large plot on the corner of Fifth Avenue and Forty-Eighth Street on which to erect a much larger headquarters for all his publishing operations—including the grandest bookstore in the city. That Scribner Building still stands unaltered (if no longer a house of books) thanks to its landmark status. It too was designed by Ernest Flagg, a more monumental variation on his earlier theme a mile and a half south on Fifth. The firm moved there a year later, in May 1913, just in time for my grandfather to go to work after his graduation. In his class yearbook he alone listed as his favorite sport "fox-hunting." He was born into books, but his chief passion was horses and riding to hounds. As an undergraduate he used to ride his horse "Mayday" thirty-five miles northward from Princeton to his family's country house, "The Gables." (Students were not allowed to keep cars in Princeton. Horses were exempt.) His identity as a publisher by birth, but a sportsman first, would later serve to forge a bond beyond the professional with his most famous author, Hemingway. But that lay far in the future.

More immediately, my grandfather's equestrian passions would prove key to my dad's—and my own—existence, for Charles III met and courted my grandmother, Vera Bloodgood Scribner, on horseback. She was equally committed to life in the saddle—in her case, sidesaddle. She would eventually become Master of the Essex Foxhounds before and during my childhood. She was called a "galloping grandmother"; there were a few others, but she ruled the field. Before she met my grandfather, whom she married in 1915, she had already broken one engagement to take off to live with her Belgian cousins, diplomats in St. Petersburg to the court of Tsar Nicholas II. That winter of 1912, she went figure skating at night with Prince Yusupov before he married the tsar's niece two years later, just before the war. He is best remembered for murdering Rasputin. But my grandmother's lasting memory was driving at night with him at breakneck speed down the streets of the city, sans headlights. "What if we run over someone?" she asked, panicked. "That's their bad luck," he replied coolly. Granny never wondered why the Russian Revolution happened.

But back to New York. My grandfather, at the time he arrived at Scribners, was a handsome young graduate who was above all a dutiful son. Early on in childhood he had displayed a keen interest, and budding talent, in art. His alarmed parents, well aware of his Flagg uncles at their easels, took away all his paints, brushes, and pens. They wanted another publisher, not a painter, in the family. He may also have been left-handed but trained to write with his right, for he had a lifelong stammer that Lillian Ross would mock in her infamous 1949 profile of Hemingway for the *New Yorker*. But for now, he was happy on Fifth, where he soon met the most important contemporary of his career: the new head of the advertising department, who had come to Scribners in 1910 right out of Harvard. In 1914—a year that would change world history for the worse and publishing history for the better—that equally striking young man would be made a Scribner editor. His name was Maxwell Perkins. The two would become inseparable at work and in friendship, all to the benefit of generations of readers.

CHAPTER 5

Dawns and Dusks

MAXWELL PERKINS DID NOT ARRIVE ALONE. THAT YEAR, 1910, also saw the arrival of another recent Harvard graduate, John Hall Wheelock. These two Harvard men invaded the predominantly Princeton domain and left a lasting imprint. I never met Perkins (he died four years before my birth), but I did get to know Wheelock, an equally gifted—even more literary if less famous—editor for half a century. The first book reception to which my father took me was for Wheelock's 1966 volume of poems, *Dear Men and Women*, at the Grolier Club. I was fourteen and home for Christmas vacation during my first year at St. Paul's. I took the inscribed book back to school with me and actually read it on the trip, the first poetry book (of the very few) I've ever read. Class poet at Harvard, Wheelock would become a distinguished poet in his own right with many awards and celebrated volumes published by Scribners over half a century. On Perkins's death in 1947 he became the house's senior editor, and he discovered and published the poets May Swenson and James Dickey—not a bad legacy.

Decades later, Dickey proved the most terrifying author I've ever met. It was at a cocktail reception at the University of South Carolina where I'd given a talk. He introduced himself, reminded me that my father had published his first book of poems, and then—fueled by several whiskeys—backed me up to the wall and asked, with all the bone-chilling intensity of his novel *Deliverance*, "What is your *ambition*?" Nonplussed, I replied, "I guess to be a good husband and father." Wrong answer. (He had been neither.) *"That* is not a worthy ambition." I'm reminded of the advice given to me by my editorial colleague Michelle Rapkin, "Charlie, if you ever especially admire an author, be sure not to meet him."

By the end of the Great War decade, Perkins would rise as the brightest literary light not only at Scribners but in all of American publishing—perhaps of all time. On the eve of America's entry into the Great War (in April 1917) Scribners published a nonfiction bestseller that remained on the bestseller lists for the final two years of that war: Alan Seeger's *Poems*—an extraordinary achievement for a young poet, alas published posthumously. He had been in T. S. Eliot's class of 1910 at Harvard, three years behind Wheelock. After moving to the Latin Quarter of Paris to pursue his art, he joined the French Foreign Legion at the outbreak of war. His most famous—and prescient—poem was "I Have a Rendezvous with Death." He was killed in battle on the Fourth of July in 1916. Scribners now had its lyrical counterpart to England's Rupert Brooke, and thanks to Wheelock, poetry would always have its place of honor in the house.

In 1917, Whitney Darrow, who had been running Princeton University Press since its founding, was called to Scribners to become a business manager for his old patron, Charles Scribner II. His long tenure at 597 Fifth Avenue was to guarantee a solid business foundation for the house, but he often clashed with the editors when his narrow commercial views of their books did not correspond to the editors' literary verdicts, expectations, and promotional plans. He could be overbearing—and often had to be overruled by CS II and later by my grandfather in order to support our most promising authors. But by the time I met him as a young boy, he was a kind, grandfatherly widower whom my parents invited over for private family dinners on Christmas Eve.

(I was still more impressed by his namesake son, Whitney Darrow Jr., the famous *New Yorker* cartoonist; from youth onward, I always gave primacy to pictures over words.)

Once—I couldn't have been more than six or seven—Mr. Darrow took me for a visit to the Scribner Building on a Saturday evening after a magic show at the University Club. It was surreal, all those dark empty offices. It would be years before I saw them buzzing with activity, punctuated by the clicks of countless typewriters on that editorial floor, the fifth—a vast open space divided by glass and wooden partitions. (No decorator would claim credit for such a spartan design, but novelist Louis Auchincloss once told my father that he considered it the most beautiful floor of offices he had ever seen.) I remember Darrow telling me that he had worked for my great-grandfather. I was impressed but also perplexed. How could anyone be that old?

When America entered the Great War, my grandfather left for France as a cavalry officer. He never saw battle—or I might not be here. But photos complete with horses prove he was close by. He returned home to 597 Fifth, but by then our most important living American novelist had left for another publisher: Edith Wharton. Ever since her 1907 affair with the unscrupulous Morton Fullerton, secretly an agent for the rival publishing house Appleton, she had played the two houses against each other for financial gain. My long-suffering great-grandfather was eager to keep her on board, for her books—her novels *The House of Mirth*, *Madame de Treymes*, *The Fruit of the Tree*, *The Custom of the Country*, *Ethan Frome*, among others, and such nonfiction delights as *Italian Villas and Their Gardens*, *Italian Backgrounds*, and *A Motor Flight Through France*—were jewels in our crown. But her lifestyle, as they call it today, always exceeded her considerable royalty earnings. By the war's end, her debt to Scribners surpassed her publisher's willingness to pay any price to keep her. She moved on to Appleton and wrote the finest novel of her long career, *The Age of Innocence*, for which in 1921 she became the first woman to win the Pulitzer Prize. But by the time I read that novel as a college student it bore the Scribner imprint. How? Because after Appleton's demise my father acquired their Wharton titles and added them all to our list. He then commissioned original paintings for his new paperback editions. And so finally all of Wharton's major novels were lined up on our shelves, as their cover paintings now do on our apartment walls, in living color. As Hemingway would famously say, "*D'abord il faut durer*" [First of all, one must endure]. Scribners endured, and in the end reclaimed the prize that got away.

Thirty years ago, I looked out our apartment window and saw a film crew—with trailers, spotlights, cameras, the works— outside the old Pyne Mansion (now the Americas Society) on Sixty-Eighth Street. It was Martin Scorsese filming his 1993 movie, *The Age of Innocence*, which would turn out to be one of the most brilliant adaptations—in this case, *operatic*—of a novel to the silver screen. It starred Daniel Day Lewis, Michelle Pfeiffer, and Winona Ryder. A year later, novelist, longtime family friend, and recent Scribner author Louis Auchincloss and I were filmed together for a BBC documentary on Wharton titled *A Lady Does Not Write*, one of the most ironic titles in the history of television. My father had commissioned Louis to write introductions for our reissues of Wharton. We were never able to be the publisher of Louis's novels, but he was our house authority on all things Wharton, whom my dad and I considered one of the finest novelists Scribners ever published. Wharton, like Jane Austen, never needed a course in "Women Writers" to be given her due. She held her own in any field.

The dusk of Wharton's departure was soon followed by the dawn of the brightest and most versatile new talent discovered— and patiently championed—by the young Max Perkins: F. Scott Fitzgerald. After leaving Princeton in 1917 before graduation and based at army training camp in Alabama, he sent the manuscript of his first novel to Perkins. It was titled *The Romantic Egotist*.

Perkins was encouraging, but it needed work, lots of it. The senior Charles was not yet persuaded to bet on the young writer. After many revisions it would at last be published in 1920, with great fanfare and glowing reviews, as *This Side of Paradise*. An instant bestseller, it launched both the twenty-four-year-old author's career and the new decade that soon came to be known as the "Jazz Age." Forgive the upcoming personal detour, but Fitzgerald deserves his own chapter—the next—for he added such a sparkling one to our family's history, from my great-grandfather's days down three successive generations to my own at our house on Fifth.

CHAPTER 6

Great Scott

F. SCOTT FITZGERALD'S LIFE AND CAREER BOUNCED BETWEEN
success and setbacks like the alternating current of major and
minor keys in a Mozart symphony. He was born in 1896, the brink
of a new century. Just as his life bridged two centuries, so does his
work have a Janus-like aspect, looking back to the Romantic lyri-
cism and epic dreams of nineteenth-century America and forward
to the syncopated jazz of the twentieth. "My whole theory of
writing," he said, "I can sum up in one sentence. An author ought
to write for the youth of his own generation, the critics of the next,
and the schoolmasters of ever afterward." How magnificently,
if posthumously, he fulfilled that ideal. His fleeting literary fortunes—a dozen years of commercial and literary success followed
by distractions and disappointments—ended in 1940 with a fatal
heart attack at the age of forty-four. He was then hard at work on
The Last Tycoon, the Hollywood novel he hoped would restore his
faded reputation. At the time of his death his books were not, as
is so often claimed, out of print with Scribners, his publisher. The
truth is even sadder: They were all in stock at our warehouse and
listed in our catalog, but no one was buying them.

When Fitzgerald's daughter, Scottie, first approached the
Princeton University Library and offered to donate her late
father's papers she was turned down. It couldn't be the repository,

the librarian said, for every failed alumnus author's papers. Fortunately she gave them a second chance, several years later, to reconsider. Today those archives are the most avidly consulted holdings of the library by scholars who come there, as if on pilgrimage, from all over the world. More copies of Fitzgerald's books are now sold each fortnight than the entire cumulative sale in his lifetime. His novels and stories are studied in high schools and colleges across the country—indeed around the world. I was the fourth Charles to be involved in publishing his works ever since my great-grandfather signed him up at the prodding of his young editor of genius Max Perkins in 1919. But three generations and namesakes later (ours is a redundant family) I am struck by the realization that mine was the first generation—of no doubt as many to come—to have been introduced to this author's work in a classroom. My grandfather, Fitzgerald's contemporary and friend as well as publisher, died on the eve of the critical reappraisal and the ensuing revival of his works that gained momentum in the 1950s and has continued in full force down to the present. It was my father who presided over that literary apotheosis unprecedented in American letters.

As a fledgling editor, I had the good fortune to work closely with Fitzgerald's delightful daughter, Scottie, together with her adviser Professor Matthew J. Bruccoli, whose prolific scholarship and infectious enthusiasm fanned the flames of Fitzgerald studies. The day I met Matt, half a century ago, I asked him what had prompted him to devote the lion's share of his scholarly life to Fitzgerald. He told me exactly how it happened.

One Sunday afternoon in 1949, Bruccoli, a high school student, was driving with his family along the Merritt Parkway from Connecticut to New York City when he heard a dramatization of "The Diamond as Big as the Ritz" on the car radio. He later went to a local library to find the story. The librarian had never heard of Scott Fitzgerald, but he finally managed to locate a copy, and "I never stopped reading Fitzgerald," he concluded. This story struck a familiar chord, for I too remember where I was when I first encountered that same literary jewel "as big as the Ritz."

It was an evening train ride from Princeton to Philadelphia—a commute was converted into a fantastic voyage. Fitzgerald later converted my professional life just as profoundly, claiming more of me than any living author. There are worse fates in publishing than to be "curator of literary classics," especially if one's own scholarly bent is in Baroque art. Placed beside my other specialties, Rubens and Bernini, Fitzgerald seems very young indeed, a newcomer in the pantheon of creative genius.

There is something magical about Fitzgerald. Much has been written—and dramatized—about the Jazz Age personas of Scott and Zelda. But the real magic lies embedded in the prose, and reveals itself in his amazing range and versatility. Each novel or story partakes of its creator's poetic imagination, his dramatic vision, his painstaking (if virtuoso and seemingly effortless) craftsmanship. Each bears Fitzgerald's hallmark: the indelible stamp of grace. He is my literary candidate to stand beside the demigods Bernini, Rubens, and Mozart as artists of divine transfigurations. The key to Fitzgerald's enduring enchantment lies, I submit, in the power of his romantic imagination to transfigure his characters and settings—as well as in the very shape and sound of his prose. There is a sacramental quality, one that did not wane along with formal observance of his Roman Catholic faith. I say "sacramental" because Fitzgerald's words transform their external geography as thoroughly as the realm within. The ultimate effect, once the initial reverberations of imagery and language have subsided, transcends the bounds of fiction. I can testify from firsthand experience.

When I arrived at Princeton as a freshman in the fall of 1969, I was following the footsteps of four generations of namesakes before me. Yet, surprisingly, I did not feel at home. It seemed a big impersonal place—more than ten times as big as my old boarding school, St. Paul's. There I had first been exposed to Fitzgerald in

English class, where we studied *The Great Gatsby*. But my first encounter at Princeton was dramatically extracurricular. One day that fall, soon after the Vietnam Moratorium and the ensuing campus turmoil, I returned to my dormitory room to find that some anonymous wit had taped to my door those infamous opening words from Fitzgerald's "The Rich Boy": "Let me tell you about the very rich. They are different from you and me." (My next-door neighbors in the dorm represented a cross-section of campus radicals, and while I was hardly "very rich" by Fitzgerald's lights—closer to Nick Carraway than to Tom Buchanan—I was, as the son of a university trustee, politically incorrect.) Stung though I was by this welcome note, curiosity got the better of me. Off I went to Firestone Library to look up the story and read it.

Now hooked on Fitzgerald, I bought a copy of *This Side of Paradise*, his youthful ode to Princeton. Though university officials to this day bemoan its satirical depiction of their college as a country club, they miss the point: the poetry, the sacramental effect of this early, flawed novel on their majestic campus. For me, this book infused the greenery and gothic spires with a spirit, with a soul, with life. Fitzgerald transfigured Princeton. I now saw it not as a stranger, but through the wondering eyes of freshman Amory Blaine:

> *Princeton of the daytime filtered slowly into his conscious-ness—West and Reunion, redolent of the sixties, Seventy-nine Hall, brick-red and arrogant, Upper and Lower Pyne, aris-tocratic Elizabethan ladies not quite content to live among shop-keepers, and topping all, climbing with clear blue aspi-ration, the great dreaming spires of Holder and Cleveland towers. From the first he loved Princeton—its lazy beauty, its half-grasped significance, the wild moonlight revel of the rushes.*

For me it was not love at first sight. But thanks to Fitzgerald, it was love at first reading. Oscar Wilde was right: Life imitates art, not the other way around. We view our world through a prism of words. During my sojourn there, friends and I would religiously recite Fitzgerald's sonnet of farewell to Princeton: "The last light fades and drifts across the land—the low, long land, the sunny land of spires."

From his earliest days, Scott wanted nothing more than to be a writer: "The first help I ever had in writing was from my father, who read an utterly imitative Sherlock Holmes story of mine and pretended to like it." It was his first appearance in print, at age thirteen. Here's the chilling dénouement (which proves that writers are made, not born):

"I forgot Mrs. Raymond," screamed Syrel, "where is she?"

"She is out of your power forever," said the young man.

Syrel brushed past him and, with Smidy and I following, burst open the door of the room at the head of the stairs. We rushed in. On the floor lay a woman, and as soon as I touched her heart I knew she was beyond the doctor's skill.

"She has taken poison," I said. Syrel looked around; the young man had gone. And we stood there aghast in the presence of death.

No surprise that he next took to writing plays, one a summer, for a local dramatics group. At Princeton, he wrote musical comedies for the Triangle Club before he flunked out (chemistry was the culprit), joined the army, and wrote his first novel, *This Side of Paradise*, which was eventually adapted to the stage as a musical under the title *The Underclassman*.

"Start out with an individual and you find that you have created a type—start out with a type and you find that you have created nothing." Fitzgerald started out with himself—a good choice. "A writer wastes nothing," he said, and he proved it by mining his early years at St. Paul and Princeton to forge his early stories, poems, and dramatic skits into that witty autobiographical novel that launched his fame.

Fitzgerald's first novel was turned down twice by my great-grandfather. But he refused to give up. Years later writing to his daughter, Fitzgerald offered the following advice: "Don't be a bit discouraged about your story not being tops. . . . Nobody became a writer just by wanting to be one. If you have anything to say, anything you feel nobody has ever said before, you have got to feel it so desperately that you will find some way to say it that nobody has ever found before."

A couple of years later, he added some more technical advice: "All fine prose is based on the verbs carrying the sentences. They make sentences move." Unlike his brisk prose, I did not move; I stayed on at Princeton for two more degrees, leaving the university only when there were no more to be had, but not before I had the pleasure of teaching undergraduates. Since my field was art history, the next transition—into the family publishing business—was abrupt, but once again facilitated by Fitzgerald.

Ensconced at Max Perkins's old desk at Scribners (which I was given because the senior editor complained that it ran her stockings) I dreamed up as my first book project in 1975 a revival of Fitzgerald's obscure and star-crossed play *The Vegetable; or from President to postman*, which featured a presidential impeachment too true to be good: the play had opened—and closed—in 1922 at Nixon's Apollo Theater in Atlantic City. My post-Watergate project not only justified repeated revisits to the Princeton University Library for research in the Scribner and Fitzgerald archives—the mecca for Fitzgerald scholars—but, more important, brought me into a happy working relationship with his daughter, Scottie. The play was republished during the election year of 1976 and featured as a presidential address a confection of mixed metaphors.

After approving my introduction to the play, Scottie wrote me a touching note about her parents' reburial service at the Catholic cemetery in Rockville, Maryland. I was unable to attend, and instead arranged for a memorial Mass to be said that day in the once exclusively Protestant Princeton chapel. No doubt Fitzgerald smiled at the delicious irony of both liturgies. "Surely it was the Princeton prayers," Scottie later wrote to me, "that made our little ceremony go so smoothly. The day was perfect; a mild breeze rustling the fallen leaves, and there were just the right number of people, about 25 friends and relatives, 25 press, 25 county and church 'officials,' and 25 admirers who just popped up from nowhere. As most of the guests had never before had Bloody Marys in a church basement, the party afterward was a jolly affair, too. I'm sorry you weren't there but loved knowing we were having a backup ceremony in his real spiritual home."

I cannot resist contrasting Scottie's gracious note with what Edmund Wilson wrote to me when I first proposed that he reintroduce the play Fitzgerald had dedicated to him. Wilson had given its publication a rave newspaper review—a fact he now conveniently chose to forget: "I cannot write an introduction to *The Vegetable*. The version I read and praised was something entirely different from the version he afterwards published, and I did not approve of this version. The trouble was he took too much advice and ruined the whole thing. I was not, by the way, as you say, closer to Fitzgerald than anybody else. I was not even in his class at college, though people still think and write as if I had been."

When I lamented this letter to my father, he said that for Wilson it wasn't so bad, jesting that "after God created the rattlesnake, he created Edmund Wilson." Not long afterward I unwittingly allowed Wilson's first name to be misspelled "Edmond" in huge letters on the cover of our paperback edition of *Axel's Castle*.

My Freudian slip is now a collector's item—which fortunately for me, Edmund did not live to see!

Fitzgerald considered his year and a half spent on *The Vegetable* a complete waste, but I disagree, for he followed it with a new novel written with all the economy and tight structure of a successful play—*The Great Gatsby*. Both *The Vegetable* and *Gatsby* shared the theme of the American Dream (first as a spoof for a comedy, finally as the leitmotif of a lyric novel). I don't think there has ever been a more elusive, mysterious, intriguing character than Gatsby. He's pure fiction—and pure Fitzgerald: the hopeful, romantic outsider looking in.

> *He smiled understandingly—much more than understandingly. It was one of those rare smiles with a quality of eternal reassurance in it that you may come across four or five times in life. It faced—or seemed to face—the whole external world for an instant, and then concentrated on you with an irresistible prejudice in your favor. It understood you just so far as you wanted to be understood, believed in you as you would like to believe in yourself and assured you that it had precisely the impression of you that, at your best, you hoped to convey.*

Who cares how James Gatz became Jay Gatsby, bootlegger or worse? Who would not want to be in such a presence? But it was years later when I met President Clinton that those sentences came to life and recorded my experience of mortal, if presidential, charisma that I could never have imagined outside the bounds of fiction. Clinton made Gatsby real. Or perhaps Gatsby prefigured Clinton?

Fitzgerald wanted his book to be a "consciously artistic achievement. . . . I want to write something new—something extraordinary and beautiful and simple + intricately patterned"— and he succeeded in spades. He later said that what he cut out of it, "both physically and emotionally, would make another novel."

In his first letter to Perkins—summer of 1922—about his "new" novel, Fitzgerald wrote that it would "concern less superlative beauties than I run to usually" and "would center on a smaller period of time." He was to change the period and locale as he began writing (it was originally set in the Midwest and New York around 1885), but he never abandoned his determination to limit the time frame and thus give a sharper focus to his plot and characters than he had done in his earlier two novels. And this, I believe, was the result of his failed attempt at being a Broadway playwright. The special demands imposed by a play—a short work defined by acts and scenes, limited in time and setting—proved an ideal exercise in literary craftsmanship, which the young novelist sharpened through the long series of revisions while the play was in rehearsal.

From Fitzgerald's long lost first draft of 1923 only a fragment survives in the form of the short story "Absolution" and two handwritten pages I discovered over four decades ago in a rare bookshop here in New York. They reveal that Fitzgerald had already settled on the essential plot and locale of the final version, but the story was told in the third person. The next year he wrote to Perkins that he was now working on a "new angle." I'm sure he meant through the eyes of his inspired narrator Nick Carraway. (It's worth streaming the famous Robert Redford film just to hear Sam Waterston tell the story—a generation before his fame in *Law & Order*.)

While writing an introduction to a new 1979 paperback edition of *Gatsby*, I decided to revive the original jacket—it is now an icon of the Jazz Age. Twenty years later it was enlarged, at my suggestion, into a huge poster for John Harbison's opera *The Great Gatsby* at the Met. When Matthew Bruccoli discovered Cugat's preliminary sketches for the Gatsby dust jacket in a country shop, serendipity allowed me at last to merge art history and literature. I'm a Gemini. For this once, thanks to Fitzgerald, my dual careers came into sync.

Francis Cugat is not a household name. Born in Spain on my birthday in 1893, he died in Connecticut on my dad's birthday in 1981. He was a set designer for Douglas Fairbanks in Hollywood and decades later a consultant to Technicolor on films including *The Quiet Man* and *The Cain Mutiny*. He is better known as the brother of bandleader Xavier Cugat. He designed only one jacket for Scribners, and did not continue in that line of work. Yet his painting is the most celebrated—and widely disseminated—jacket art in twentieth-century American literature, and perhaps of all time. After decades of oblivion, and several million copies later, like the novel it embellishes, this Art Deco tour de force has established itself as a classic of graphic art. At the same time, it represents a unique form of "collaboration" between author and jacket artist. Under normal circumstances, the artist illustrates a scene or motif conceived by the author; he lifts, as it were, his image from a page of the book. In this instance, however, the artist's image preceded the finished manuscript and Fitzgerald actually maintained that he had "written it into" his book.

Cugat's small masterpiece is not illustrative, but symbolic, iconic. The sad, hypnotic, heavily outlined eyes of a woman beam like headlights through a cobalt night sky. Below, on earth, brightly colored lights blaze before a metropolitan skyline. Cugat's carnival imagery is especially intriguing in view of Fitzgerald's pervasive use of light motifs throughout his novel, specifically in metaphors for the latter-day Trimalchio, whose parties were illuminated by "enough colored lights to make a Christmas tree of Gatsby's enormous garden." Nick sees "the whole corner of the peninsula . . . blazing with light" from Gatsby's house, "lit from tower to cellar." When he tells Gatsby that his place "looks like the World's Fair," Gatsby proposes that they "go to Coney Island." Fitzgerald had already introduced this symbolism in his story "Absolution," originally intended as a prologue to the novel. At the end of the story, a priest encourages the boy who eventually developed into Jay Gatsby to go see an amusement park, "a thing like a fair only much more glittering" with "a big wheel made of lights turning in the air." But "don't get too close," he cautions, "because if you do you'll only feel the heat and the sweat and the life."

Daisy's face, says Nick, was "sad and lovely with bright things in it, bright eyes and a bright passionate mouth." In Cugat's final painting, her celestial eyes enclose reclining nudes and her streaming tear is green—like the light "that burns all night" at the end of her dock, reflected in the water of the sound that separates her from Gatsby. What Fitzgerald drew directly from Cugat's art and "wrote into" the novel must ultimately remain an open question, though I believe the best candidate is not the famous billboard eyes of Dr. T. J. Eckleburg but rather Nick's image of Daisy, at the end of chapter 4, as "the girl whose disembodied face floated along the dark cornices and blinding signs" of New York at night.

The reflected lights and ghosts of Gatsby—whether votive or festive—still transfigure Gatsby's Island, where my family and I were transplanted in the mid-1980s after several generations on the mainland side of the Hudson River. From our new vantage point, I cannot look out over the sound without smiling at Fitzgerald's description: "the most domesticated body of saltwater in the western hemisphere, the great wet barnyard of Long Island Sound." There is no longer a dock at the beach in Lattingtown, and, as the crow flies, we are in fact several miles east of East Egg. But occasionally I catch a glimpse of a green light reflected in the water, and each time I drive through the Valley of Ashes (now the site of the Citi Field stadium) and approach the twinkling Manhattan skyline, I feel very much at home. The novel has made me a native.

One wise college professor told us that the ultimate function of art is to reconcile us to life. Fitzgerald's prose is life enhancing; its evocative power endures. That is why I have no doubt he should be beaming still—from the other side of Paradise.

CHAPTER 7

Editor Maximus

F. SCOTT FITZGERALD'S AUSPICIOUS DEBUT WAS IMMEDIATELY followed by a collection of stories, *Flappers and Philosophers* (1920), then a second—and much underrated—semi-autobiographical novel of romance, wildlife, and dissipation: *The Beautiful and Damned* (1922). Set mainly in Westport, Connecticut—where newlyweds Scott and Zelda, expelled from their first-class hotel in New York, rented a house for five months and partied through the nights—it was a commercial and critical disappointment: too loosely structured, meandering through a shimmering haze of bootleg gin. Half a century later, British playwright Christopher Isherwood would write a screenplay of the novel with Perry King, editor Max Perkins's grandson, in mind as the star.

That summer in Westport would eventually set the stage for his greatest novel, *Gatsby*, published three years later, after another volume of stories aptly titled *Tales of the Jazz Age* (1922) and his ill-fated play *The Vegetable* (1923), with which he honed the craft of concision. Their Westport cottage would soon be transplanted as Nick Carraway's across the sound, along with the extravagant parties of their mysterious millionaire neighbor F. E. Lewis. But that was not to be discovered for almost a century. When this novel hypothesis—that the origins of Gatsby and "West Egg" lay in Westport—was first proposed by Richard Webb Jr. (and later published in his 2018 book *Boats Against the Current*) my initial response, on Facebook, was one word: "Poppycock!" But I soon had to take it back. I was converted—as suddenly as St. Paul—by their convincing discoveries and arguments, to the point that I signed on as executive producer for their 2020 documentary film *Gatsby in Connecticut* featuring the actor Sam Waterston, who had played to perfection narrator Nick Carraway in the 1974 film.

That documentary is well worth watching, for it illustrates the magic of metamorphosis—in this case, geographical transfusion—in the hands of that most gifted novelist. At the time, back in the mid-1920s, Scott was earning huge sums (approaching seven figures in today's dollars) by writing and selling his short stories to the popular "glossy" magazines, stories that both defined and celebrated the Jazz Age. He and Zelda then moved to Paris with their young daughter, Scottie—a geographical cure that proved providential for Scribners. In Paris while completing *Gatsby*, he met a fellow American expatriate who was trying to make his mark as a writer: Ernest Hemingway. In a famous telegram of 1924, Fitzgerald cabled his editor Max Perkins to look up this promising young writer "with a brilliant future." He misspelled the name as "Hemmingway," but no matter; it was to prove the most profitable introduction in our history.

That same year, Perkins published the first of many books by another Fitzgerald pal, the satirist and sportswriter Ring Lardner Jr. Young Hemingway had been such a fan of Lardner that in his high school newspaper he penned his sports articles under the pseudonym "Ring Lardner." Every budding baseball player should read his classic story "Alibi Ike."

In May 1926 Hemingway made a quiet splash with *The Torrents of Spring*—a transparent satire of Sherwood Anderson written to break his prior contract with Anderson's publisher Boni & Liveright—and then a bigger splash in October with *The Sun Also Rises*. That banner year belongs to Hemingway, as the previous one does to Fitzgerald and *Gatsby*. The following year brought forth a second collection of Fitzgerald stories, *All the Sad Young Men*, and John Galsworthy's *The Silver Spoon*, one of the several sequels to his monumental *Forsyte Saga*, published in 1922. That saga, which as a prep school Anglophile I found so intoxicating, was adapted to the television screen in a 1967 BBC series (twenty-six episodes in all) and repeated the next year on Sunday nights with such success that some eighteen million British viewers tuned in for the final episode. It crossed the Atlantic, and its wild American success in 1969 would soon set the stage on Sunday nights for the series *Masterpiece Theatre*, the crown of public television for the past half century.

In the United Kingdom, on Sunday nights people had regretted dinner invitations, pubs closed, and evensong church services were canceled. Across the Atlantic, I commuted home each Sunday, either to my parents or my Scribner grandmother (she had known Galsworthy, which added to my enjoyment) in order not to miss an episode. It was broadcast in glorious black and white, yet in memory it eclipses the blockbusters that followed, from *Upstairs/Downstairs* to *Downton Abbey*.

In 1926 the firm also published Will James's *Smoky, the Cowhorse*, which won the Newbery Medal for the best illustrated children's book. I still cherish the horse illustration he drew for my father as a boy, now safely preserved in a scrapbook. Perhaps my grandparents hoped it would encourage their son to pursue a life on horseback. It didn't. Dad was allergic to horses. That same month of Hemingway's rising *Sun*, October, saw the dawn of another series, this time of murder mysteries, with the publication of *The Benson Murder Case* by S. S. Van Dine, a pseudonym for the art critic Willard Huntington Wright. This avant-garde critic had suffered a breakdown from "overwork" (actually a cocaine addiction) and during his long recuperation had taken to reading hundreds of detective novels for relaxation. He soon decided that he could do better. So he gave to his friend from Harvard days, Max Perkins, an outline of three murder mysteries to be solved by a rich, snobbish, aesthete-playing-sleuth in Jazz Age New York City named Philo Vance, a worthy American counterpart to Dorothy Sayers's Lord Peter Wimsey.

Followed by *The Canary Murder Case* and *The Greene Murder Case*, the series eventually comprised a dozen books, all of which I read in my youth (along with all of Ian Fleming's James Bond series; when it came to literature I was more addict than highbrow). They were instant successes and soon turned into famous films as well as bestsellers that made their author rich. They later would be favorite reading among our officers in the POW camps during World War II. Shortly after my young dad took over as head of the company in 1952, he got a phone call from a Hollywood producer who wanted to know the title of the most recent Philo Vance mystery; they all had been made into films. My dad paused for a moment and then replied, "*The Gracie Allen Murder Case.*"

The producer was nonplussed, "Oh, no, no, no, I know the *Gracie Allen*. I want the newest, the *last* one." When my dad replied, "That *is* the last one," the Hollywood mogul exclaimed, "It *can't* be. What happened?"

"What happened is simple: The author died." To which the producer countered with utter incredulity, "Well, you didn't have to let the *series* die, did you?" Publishing had entered a new era.

But back in the Roaring Twenties, Scribners was also publishing some memorable—some less so—books in nonfiction. The prize surely goes to an Englishman of eloquent literary and oratorical powers that would eventually win a war: Winston Churchill. In 1923, the first two of his five-volume history on the Great War, *The World Crisis*, came out. It would take eight years to complete. Scribners' advance (payment of royalties) to Churchill in 1921 enabled him to buy a new Rolls-Royce. The next year he bought his famous country estate, Chartwell. The history was well received to many glowing reviews, though some contemporaries took umbrage at the author's egotism. Former Prime Minister

Arthur Balfour, who had served as Foreign Secretary during the First World War (and set the stage for the eventual State of Israel), described it as "autobiography disguised as a history of the universe." But Churchill was embraced by Scribners wholeheartedly, and soon became a favorite drinking pal of my grandfather on their visits together here and abroad.

Before the series was published in full, Churchill followed up with a real autobiography, a classic that I first read in English class as a new student at St. Paul's and has remained a favorite ever since, *My Early Life: A Roving Commission*. Soon after Scribners published our one-volume abridgment of *The World Crisis* in 1992, I sent a copy to former president Richard Nixon, to whom I'd earlier sent our new biography of Woodrow Wilson. He was a huge admirer of both world leaders, as well as of Teddy Roosevelt. In a most gracious handwritten reply, Nixon noted that he had read the original volumes many years earlier. Then, with an insight unimaginable from any former president save Harry Truman (his peer as a voracious reader of history), he added, "Incidentally, I believe the final volume on 'The Eastern Front' was the best. Churchill is better when he writes about events in which he did not play a role." Finally, he responded to my complaint about Churchill bashers among recent historians with typical Nixonian flair: "I am disgusted, as you are, by those who try to tarnish his reputation. They will not succeed."

The decade drew to its close with an unusual book that as a fledgling editor I discovered tucked away on a shelf in our fifth-floor editorial library. On its jacket was printed a bold signed and dated inscription (in longhand) by Il Duce himself: "There is no other autobiography by me—Benito Mussolini." True enough, but only half the story. The 1928 book was dictated to our former ambassador to Italy, Richard Washburn Child, who wrote the introduction, and then ghost-written by Child and a young Italian journalist named Luigi Barzini Jr., who would later become most famous for his 1964 bestseller, *The Italians*. In 1940 Barzini was arrested as anti-Fascist (for selling secrets to the enemy) and placed under house arrest; he was finally liberated in 1944 by American GIs. All's well that ends well.

In 1929 we brought to the reading public a far more authentic and lasting book set in Italy: Hemingway's *A Farewell to Arms*. It remains for many his most beloved novel. It was also his first bestseller. Three years later it was made into a Hollywood film starring Helen Hayes and Gary Cooper, who would become one of the author's closest friends for the rest of his life. Remade in Technicolor in 1957 and starring Rock Hudson and Jennifer Jones, it hit television a decade later as one of the early miniseries, in three parts. But 1929 also witnessed the debut of the author most closely associated with Perkins as "editor of genius": Thomas Wolfe. His massive novel—even after Perkins's painstaking pruning of some sixty thousand words—bore the poetic title *Look Homeward, Angel.* That autobiographical coming-of-age "sensation," as one review dubbed this classic set in a fictionalized Asheville, North Carolina, took the literary world by storm. The film *Genius* (2016) tells the tortured tale of its publication more vividly than I dare, or need, attempt here. My dad told me it's a novel best read young; I missed my chance—long ago.

If 1929 is remembered above all for the stock market crash that precipitated the Great Depression, at Scribners it marked a crash that didn't happen. That year we published the most controversial biography in our history: Edwin Dakin's *Mrs. Eddy: The Biography of a Virginal Mind*, a meticulously researched account of the founder of Christian Science that exposed her as a delusional charlatan (while crediting her business acumen) with a healthy morphine habit, among other colorful traits. It was praised in the press for its objectivity and thoroughness, but the Mother Church was not amused. It did everything in its power to suppress the book: threatening bookstores with mortgage foreclosures, stealing copies off shelves, even threatening the publisher with "malicious animal magnetism," according to editor John Hall Wheelock.

Many bookstores hid their copies to prevent shoplifting by church emissaries. Scribner's Bookstore (since it was owned by the publisher) did the opposite: We put it front and center in a huge display. When the bookstore manager reported in a panic to my great-grandfather threats to smash those plate glass windows on Fifth if the books were not removed, Scribner responded: "Leave them where they are. We have insurance." There was no crashing glass. In fact, the campaign to suppress the book made it a bestseller. It was republished a year later with an accompanying booklet titled "The Blight That Failed."

After marking fifty years at the helm of Scribners in 1928, CS II decided to retire. Perhaps the publication of Galsworthy's bestseller *Swan Song*, number-three bestseller that year, may have supplied some solace, if not a hint. Before year-end, the first of twenty-one volumes of *The Dictionary of American Biography* (which would be completed within a decade) appeared, a tremendous achievement and promise of future prestige in publishing reference works, those crown jewels that reflected his father's and his own earlier achievements with the twenty-five volumes of Lange's biblical *Commentary* and later the *Encyclopedia Britannica* of the previous century—with one big difference: The *DAB*, as it was called in-house and at universities and libraries, was *created* by Scribners overseeing its team of contributing scholars.

Developed in collaboration with the American Council of Learned Societies, which would later partner with Scribners on other reference projects under my father, the *DAB* was the most important project the firm had ever undertaken. As such, it became the prototype for many more such monuments of research published out of the Scribner offices. Charles II, now called "Old CS" (*sotto voce*), could rest on his laurels as he turned over the presidency to his younger brother, Arthur, and stayed on only as chairman of the board. Well, "only" is not quite the right word. Old CS continued to interfere in every aspect of the house. Sometimes he would appear unannounced and "out of retirement" at the offices to nullify decisions made by Arthur. It must have been difficult, if familiar: Older brothers never change their spots. When he died at age seventy-five (the oldest of all our Charleses to the present day) on April 19, 1930, Arthur was finally in undisputed charge for the next two years until his own death on July 3, 1932. Three junior family members were under Arthur at the firm: Scribner Fitzhugh (son of Isabelle, Charles and Arthur's youngest sister), Arthur's nephew Charles III (my grandfather, not me; the recycling of numerals has caused considerable confusion), and his great-nephew George McKay Schieffelin, who later became my godfather.

If Uncle Arthur's tenure after his brother's death was brief, it was not uneventful. In 1930, as if to counterbalance the eminently forgettable Fascist autobiography of two years earlier, Scribners published *My Life* by Leon Trotsky. The Russian revolutionary and Bolshevik and Communist leader had written it while in Turkey after being expelled from the party as an anti-Stalinist. (He would eventually be assassinated by a Stalinist agent in Mexico in 1940.) Yet he continued to sign all his letters to Scribners, today in the Princeton archives, in red ink. From 1930 to 1932 the house boasted several bestsellers, from Will James's *Lone Cowboy* (1930) to Galsworthy's *Maid in Waiting* (1931) and Clarence Darrow's *The Story of My Life* (1932), all of which were still selling on our list a half century later when I was publisher of our paperback division.

Five months after Charles II's death, our London office moved to a more spacious townhouse near the British Museum at 23 Bedford Square, which was fast becoming the new publishing headquarters in the city. In January of 1932, *Scribner's Magazine* released its new, larger format with full-color covers in line with *Life*, *Look*, and *The Saturday Evening Post*, along with other glossy competitors. Marcia Davenport made her debut that year with the first English-language biography of Mozart, my favorite composer, still in print today. She was to become Max Perkins's most worshipful of authors among the new roster of the female best-selling novelists he launched into print.

At the other end of the scale, in 1931 under Arthur's aegis Scribners published the shortest book in our history, twelve pages in all: *Laws of Backgammon*, authored by the newly formed Backgammon and Cards Committee of his club a few blocks away, the Racquet and Tennis Club, which my grandfather, father, and I would consider our favorite daily sanctuary from office life. (On one rare occasion when my father took an author to lunch there, he wrote the scene into his next novel, describing this unnamed club as having waiters who looked like the directors of any other club.) This slim booklet looms large in my memory since the club recently asked me to arrange for its republication. Its very existence was news to me. I hadn't played the game since college, but that didn't stop me from writing the foreword for this new paperback edition. It was an enlightening research project; I had no idea the game dated back five thousand years to Mesopotamia. As my dad first reassured me when I first undertook a history of Scribners in my twenties, "Just remember, Charlie, everyone has been young; not everyone has been old." I find that comment, whatever it means, even more encouraging as time moves on.

CHAPTER 8

A Horseman Takes the Reins

THE DEATH OF HIS UNCLE ON JULY 3, 1932—THE YEAR FRANK-lin D. Roosevelt was sworn in as our new US president—left my grandfather, Charles Scribner III, to take the reins at Scribners solo. He was forty-two years old, with a teenage daughter, Julia, and his ten-year-old son, Charlie, at home in Far Hills, New Jersey. He made the over-two-hour commute each way every weekday—by car to the railroad, then the Hudson tube and New York City subway. On the weekends he fox-hunted. It would be hard to think of a tougher time at which to take over the management of a large publishing house. The Great Depression was in its worst stage and the future must have seemed most uncertain for books. Hemingway's new title that year—and his first nonfiction book—on bullfighting, might have given his publisher pause: *Death in the Afternoon*. (His next title, for a collection of short stories already in the works for the following year, *Winner Take Nothing*, was hardly more encouraging.) But faith would have the last word, for 1932 would conclude with *Moral Man and Immoral Society*, the first of many religious titles to follow by that towering theologian, ethicist, and eventual consultant for the firm's religion list: Reinhold Niebuhr. My father would later list that title among the five that had meant most to him.

When Arthur's widow, Helen, died nineteen years later she left everything to Princeton. While I approved of her generosity, I asked my father why she hadn't left something to her nephew, my grandfather, since she and Uncle Arthur were childless. He explained that there had been an unfortunate misunderstanding immediately following his uncle's death. During their marriage, Arthur had been bringing home to his wife a twenty-dollar gold piece each week (think five hundred dollars today). He called it a "dividend." After his death, Helen came in to see her nephew, now in charge, and asked for her "dividend," which of course she had ceased receiving. My grandfather, knowing nothing about his uncle's habit, explained to her that the company never paid dividends. Aunt Helen was sure he had pulled a fast one on her, and never forgot it.

Meanwhile, Scribners continued to look for fresh talent and take chances on new authors in a way that would mark this decade as one of the most enterprising in all our history, an achievement that testifies to the aims and courage of Charles III and to the devoted support that his colleagues—Max Perkins above all—gave him. They had become fast friends at work and dined together every day in those days of three-martini lunches. In the following years many important new works appeared on our lists, not only by the already big names Fitzgerald, Hemingway, and Wolfe, but also by relatively unknown writers who would later become famous after their auspicious debuts. The next year marked the debut of another outstanding writer: Marjorie Kinnan Rawlings with *South Moon Under*. It would be followed five years later by the number-one bestseller of 1938 and Pulitzer Prize winner for 1939, *The Yearling*, a favorite book I read as a child in its Scribner Illustrated Classics edition with paintings by N. C. Wyeth.

Rawlings was an extraordinary talent—and woman. Her hardscrabble, adventurous life in Florida's frontier country was chronicled in her memoir, *Cross Creek*, a decade later; her home there is now a National Landmark. Fifty years after her Scribner debut, my wife and I attended, together with Marjorie's widower, Norton Baskin, the premiere of the magnificent film *Cross Creek*, starring Mary Steenburgen as Rawlings and Peter Coyote as Baskin. Malcolm McDowell played Max Perkins, who gamely traveled there to encourage and guide his most remote new author. It's even better than *Genius*, the more recent Perkins film, a must-see for anyone interested in the alchemy between editor and author.

Rawlings soon became a close friend not only of her fellow Scribner novelist Marcia Davenport but, even closer to home, to my Aunt Julia. They became fast friends, confidantes, and correspondents. A rich volume of their letters over the decades was published in 2022, and it reveals the extent to which Rawlings became a surrogate mother to my aunt, her publisher's elder child. Rawlings had had a difficult relationship with her own mother and saw in young Julia a girl who was experiencing some of the same challenges. She eventually sent Julia the manuscript of her unpublished first novel, *Blood of My Blood*, as a way of illuminating their shared experiences as daughters. Eventually Marjorie named Aunt Julia her literary executor. In the eight years between Rawlings's death in 1953 (at age fifty-seven) and her own untimely death at age forty-three, my aunt oversaw posthumous publications of Rawlings and edited for my father an anthology: *The Marjorie Rawlings Reader*.

In 1987 the sole copy of Rawlings's *Blood of My Blood* manuscript was discovered by one of my cousins in the attic of their family farmhouse in New Marlborough, Massachusetts. I arranged for them to have it sold to a collector and scholar interested in teaching and eventually publishing it. The existence of the manuscript was news to Rawlings's widower, Norton Baskin, and to the University of Florida, the designated beneficiary and custodian of all the author's papers. They were convinced that they had been cheated out of the manuscript. (I had, and have to this day, no doubts. My aunt was as scrupulous as her brother; she would never have confused papers entrusted to her as an executor with a personal gift to her from Rawlings.) Lawsuits ensued as my late aunt's ownership of the manuscript was challenged. But in the end, a truce was called and the book was finally published in 2002 by the university. Case closed.

The year after Rawlings's debut on the Scribner list, 1934, saw the publication (and serialization in *Scribner's Magazine*) of Fitzgerald's new novel, *Tender Is the Night*, nine years after his last one, *Gatsby*. It cost him almost a decade of labor and private pain, as Zelda's mental condition declined and required extended stays in hospitals. The novel, Fitzgerald's own favorite, captures all that tragedy in the characters of Nicole and Dick Diver. By the time of its publication the author had lost his battle to save Zelda from mental illness and their marriage from the inevitable consequences. The novel was as much a product of Scott's experience of struggle and heartbreak as his credo in fidelity, perseverance, and romantic love. It would remain, despite uneven reviews and disappointing initial sales, one of his most beloved works because it rings absolutely true, because it *is* true. Among its early fans was Rawlings, who found it "disturbing, bitter, and beautiful":

> *I am totally unable to analyze the almost overpowering effect that some of his passages create. . . . There is something terrifying about it when it happens, and the closest I can come to understanding it is to think that he does, successfully at such times, what I want to do—that is, visualizes people not in their immediate setting, from the human point of view—but in time and space—almost, you might say, with divine detachment.*

But the most illuminating appraisal or "review" of all is found in Fitzgerald's own inscription in a friend's copy of the novel: "If you liked *The Great Gatsby*, for God's sake read this. *Gatsby* was a tour de force, but this is a confession of faith."

That summer of '34 Scribners published to rave reviews what has been called "the best and most completely realized novel of the Deep South in the Civil War": Stark Young's *So Red the Rose*, set in the Natchez region of Mississippi. If it was soon eclipsed two years later by Mitchell's *Gone with the Wind*, it has held its place in the Southern literary firmament, with several editions still in print. Its author was also a painter, as the title may hint, and our family has two of his floral oil paintings, given to his publisher and wife, on our walls.

In October of the same year, my grandfather published the first two (of four) volumes of Douglas Southall Freeman's *R. E. Lee: A Biography*, a bestseller that won the 1935 Pulitzer Prize for biography. Somehow I don't think such a comprehensive and sympathetic biography of the Confederate general would be a candidate today. But then, what publisher now would have paid (in today's buying power) upward of a million dollars for Churchill's four-volume biography of his warrior ancestor John Churchill, the first Duke of Marlborough, who was rewarded for his victory over the French at the Battle of Blenheim with a palace, where the author was born? It was published over five years, from 1933 to 1938, by which time new clouds of war were gathering over Britain. If it didn't earn out Scribners' advance, at least in hindsight we can take solace in the thought that the company contributed to the successful outcome of the Second World War by supporting Britain's future prime minister—and indispensable war leader—at a time when he depended on his writing income to support himself (in the manner, it must be said, to which he was born) during those years out of office.

After Churchill's death in 1965 American political philosopher Leo Strauss wrote, "Not a whit less important than his deeds and speeches are his writings, above all his *Marlborough*—the greatest historical work written in our century, an inexhaustible mine of political wisdom and understanding, which should be required reading for every student of political science." My father later made that easier: He had the volumes abridged by American historian Henry Steele Commager and reissued in one volume. Even more important to the biography's afterlife, following its author's death, was the 1969 BBC series *The First Churchills* (in twelve episodes), which followed *The Forsyte Saga* on PBS and in 1971 launched *Masterpiece Classic*—later called *Masterpiece Theatre*—in the States. I watched every episode with my parents. My father had anticipated its success by reissuing in 1968 the Commager abridgment in four volumes as a boxed paperback Scribner Library set. And so that massive biography enjoyed a late revival in that life beyond life to which all authors aspire. Churchill must have been beaming.

By 1934 it had become clear to my grandfather that the house needed a professional department of children's books. Up until that time there had been no formal distinction between children's books and adult books at the house; juvenile books were simply considered a part of general books. Recalling the successes of *Peter Pan* and perhaps the near miss of *The Wind in the Willows*, CS III set up the new department with Alice Dalgliesh as its founding editor. She proceeded to build one of the most distinguished lists of children's books in American publishing. She was also a celebrated author herself and would go on to pen over three dozen children's books, the first Scribner books I came to know and love: *The Silver Pencil, The Bears on Hemlock Mountain, The Courage of Sarah Noble, The Columbus Story, The Thanksgiving Story, The Fourth of July Story*—you get the idea. It is fair to say that "Miss Dalgliesh," as I knew her from my earliest years, shaped my view of national holidays. She was also my favorite editor to visit with my dad at the office. In his own memoir, my father summed her up best: "She was a professional through and through. Indeed she gave me my real education in publishing as a business, as a set of obligations, and as a career requiring the highest standards." She was without a doubt my grandfather's most valuable hire, as well as the first female editor at Scribners. But the story would not be complete without a footnote my father later shared privately with me.

Miss Dalgliesh had been in her new post upstairs for three or four days before she went to see my grandfather in his corner office on the fifth floor. He liked her very much and asked how she was getting on.

"Oh, just fine, Mr. Scribner, but there is one thing I'd like."

"Of course," he said, "What is it?"

"Do you think I might have a desk?"

"Well, yes, I don't see why not, of course you can. It just never occurred to us you'd need one."

And so with Alice Dalgliesh the women's movement dawned at 597 Fifth Avenue.

The next year, 1935, was a banner one for books, including Hemingway's second nonfiction work, *Green Hills of Africa*, about his recent safari, and a new collection of short stories by Fitzgerald, *Taps at Reveille*—a telling title in view of his recent years of struggles; he would die much too young five years later. But the big book, in every sense, that year was Thomas Wolfe's massive novel *Of Time and the River*. The sprawling manuscript, which had arrived in crates and was originally conceived to require several volumes, à la Proust, was soon subjected to major surgery by Max Perkins, whom Wolfe viewed as a confidant, champion, and even surrogate father. It was without question the Herculean labor of Perkins's career at the desk I later inherited. On one occasion Wolfe, bruised by the surgery in process, came into Max's office and spotted on the desk an ashtray fashioned in the shape of a coiled rattlesnake, given to Perkins by the Western writer Will James. Pointing to it, Wolfe solemnly announced: "Portrait of an editor."

Yet Wolfe prefaced his new novel with an over-the-top dedication suggesting that Max had played the critical, if not chief, role in its final form. He had so often said to others that he couldn't have written his books without Max.

To Maxwell Evarts Perkins

A great editor and a brave and honest man, who stuck by the writer of this book through times of bitter hopelessness and doubt and would not let him give into his own despair, a work to be known as "Of Time and the River" is dedicated with the hope that all of it may be in some way worthy of the loyal devotion and the patient care which a dauntless and unshaken friend has given to each part of it, and without which none of it could have been written.

Perkins, by nature a shy and self-effacing man, was deeply embarrassed by Wolfe's hyperbolic tribute; indeed he was to pay a bitter price for it when Wolfe soon after decided he had to prove—to himself, to the critics, and the public—that he could write a book without Max. After penning several stormy and reproachful letters, Wolfe left Perkins and Scribners. His last books were to be published by Harper & Brothers—posthumously, as it turned out—and with the final irony that Perkins, whom Wolfe had appointed his literary executor, had to oversee their publication personally.

Perkins kept Wolfe's angry letters buried in his desk, where they were found only after his death. Evidently he could not bear to have his colleagues see the dark side of the author's personality. The desk was cleaned out several times after it passed to successive senior editors John Hall Wheelock and Burroughs Mitchell before I inherited it. All the original contents had by then found their way into our archives at Princeton—almost. One day, irritated that a drawer would not close completely, I removed the drawer to see what was blocking it. I reached into a half century of dust to find two crumpled sheets of paper clipped to a photograph. Not exactly buried treasure, at least not at first sight.

The battered photograph was of Thomas Wolfe, a photo of his portrait by Douglas Gorsline, with a note by Wolfe's agent Elizabeth Nowell: "This is Max Perkins's *only* personal copy. Please *be sure* not to mark or deface it in any way." The accompanying sheets of paper were a typescript poem titled, in a very rough hand, "Last Poem," with "Brooklyn (1934)" inscribed below the title. It took no Sherlock Holmes to deduce its authorship. Aside from the circumstantial evidence of desk and photo, the impassioned poetic voice and baroque imagery were as telltale as the frenzied handwriting. The next week I gave the poem its first public reading at a party we were hosting, by pure coincidence, for the Thomas Wolfe Society in our editorial library where Wolfe had spent many a night sleeping on the floor; he had wanted to read all his publisher's books, he explained. This literary giant did *everything* to excess, even once helping himself to a huge bowl of "stew" at my grandparents' house in Far Hills in the middle of a Homeric night of drinking with another houseguest. The next morning my grandmother, who was raising a dozen show dogs, cairn terriers, heard the panicked cook scream from the kitchen, "What happened to all the dog food?"

After that ceremonial reading, I gave the poem to join our other treasures in the Princeton University Library and then published it along with my tale in an early issue of the revived *Vanity Fair* (1983). As Fitzgerald wrote in his first novel, "If it wasn't life, it was magnificent." Max's desk soon followed. It now rests in the university librarian's office.

The Spanish-born George Santayana's novel *The Last Puritan* won us the silver in 1936 as the year's number-two bestseller. To be beaten only by *Gone with the Wind* was cause enough for celebration. Has any Harvard professor of philosophy done better in fiction? My father's favorite Santayana quotation, which he gave me to ponder as a student, was from his poem "A Poet's

Testament": "I give back to the earth what the earth gave / All to the furrow, none to the grave." It still echoes in the mind's ear.

The year would close with two major contributions to scholarship.

The first was the great German Protestant theologian Paul Tillich's *The Interpretation of History*. Tillich had left his native land after the Nazi takeover in 1933, settled in New York, and was now a colleague of Niebuhr's at Union Theological Seminary. He would go on to publish many more titles with Scribners, and even from my Catholic perspective I consider him the greatest light in our history of religious publishing, which would soon include such giants in theology, sacred history, and biblical studies as Rudolf Bultmann, Joachim Jeremias, Martin Buber, Jacques Maritain, Etienne Gilson, and Fulton J. Sheen (our only author who is up for canonization). Tillich would later become the subject of my senior independent study in a private seminar at St. Paul's School, and twenty-five years later the subject of the first book Michelle Rapkin and I commissioned for our revived program of religious publishing after Scribners merged with Macmillan in 1984. But back to 1936, which concluded with the announced plans for our next major reference work, *The Dictionary of American History*, edited by historian John Truslow Adams.

My own favorite milestone of that year, however, was Marcia Davenport's first novel: *Of Lena Geyer*. If now obscure, it remains the finest novel ever written about an opera singer, indeed about the world of opera in the Golden Age, for it drew deep from its author's vast musical knowledge as a critic and her creative instincts as a born novelist. Marcia's mother was the legendary Metropolitan Opera soprano Alma Gluck, who had famously sung opposite Caruso and was one of the first classical artists to sell a million copies of a phonograph record in the United States. (She is also the mother of actor Efrem Zimbalist Jr.) Our author of *Mozart* wrote a fictional biography of a diva so compelling and authentic that for decades to come the Met's press office received letters addressed to "Lena Geyer." Over thirty years later, it would have a profound impact on me personally and professionally in my relationship with its author. But I must leave that operatic score for later—there's a limit to digressions.

While he was abroad covering the Spanish Civil War as a correspondent for the American Newspaper Alliance, Hemingway published two books with Scribners. The first was the 1937 novel *To Have and Have Not*, about Harry Morgan, a cynical runner of guns, men, and rum between Cuba and Key West during the Depression, where Hemingway was living with his wife Pauline and their sons when not covering the civil war in Spain. Burdened with a heavy dose of Marxist ideology, which the author had absorbed from the Spanish Republicans with whom he sympathized, it failed to attain the critical and commercial success of *A Farewell to Arms*. The *New York Times* reviewer concluded that "Mr. Hemingway's record as a creative writer would be stronger if it had never been published." While the book was in progress, two years earlier, Perkins got his own dose of life at sea with Hemingway. On one fishing outing in the Gulf Stream, the two got caught in a major storm. As it grew more and more threatening, Hemingway found his "grace under pressure" sorely tested, especially as Max remained cool and seemingly unconcerned with the mortal danger they were facing. Finally Hemingway lost it and snapped at his editor, "Max, it's all very well for you to sit there so calmly. You have five daughters and don't care whether you live or not!"

If more sympathetically viewed today as a novel of ideas rendered with crisp realism by the master of the genre, it remains eclipsed by the film adaptation in 1944. At the height of World War II, the location was transplanted from the Gulf Stream to Vichy France, with Harry Morgan played by Humphrey Bogart, who met his costar, nineteen-year-old Lauren Bacall, making her debut on the set. She would soon become his fourth and final wife. Their son Stephen was a school friend of mine in New York;

his deceased father by then a legend, and his mother a major star. Perhaps that is why, for me, the film outshone our novel. In any case, the novel was followed a year later, in 1938, by a major collection of Hemingway short stories: *The Fifth Column and Forty-Nine Stories*. His next bestseller would within two years reestablish his place at the pinnacle of American fiction.

But it was a woman, not Hemingway, who won the gold for Scribners in 1938: Marjorie Kinnan Rawlings, with *The Yearling*, the year's number-one bestseller and the 1939 winner of the Pulitzer Prize for fiction. Whitney Darrow, then head of the trade (general books) department, objected to its being published as an adult book. Fortunately he was overruled. It too would become not only a beloved Scribner Illustrated Classic but a major film (1946) starring Gregory Peck and Jane Wyman, the first wife of future President Reagan.

The next year, 1939, a darkening one for Europe and soon the world, gained Scribners another Pulitzer, this time in drama, with *Abe Lincoln in Illinois* by Robert E. Sherwood; it was his second in three years. A month later, my grandfather was named the sponsor of book and magazine publishers for the New York World's Fair. But his own magazine would fold in May, a casualty to slicker mass-market competition. It had its day—for fifty years, not a bad run. By the year's end, war had broken out between Nazi Germany and the Allies, France and Britain. The following May, after the election of Scribner author Churchill as prime minister, the head of our London office returned home to the States. His place was taken at Bedford Square by thirty-five-year-old John Carter, a graduate of Eton and King's College, Cambridge. After serving with the British Information Service during the war years he would return to Scribners to become managing director before moving to Washington, in 1953, as personal assistant to Her Majesty's ambassador for three years. The author himself of several books about rare books, he lent luster to our English branch.

By the fall, the Battle of Britain was raging in full force as it neared its end; it had claimed the life of my mother's twenty-two-year-old first cousin Peter Pease, eldest son of Sir Richard and Lady Pease of Richmond, Yorkshire, one of the most celebrated heroes of the Royal Air Force during those darkest hours. He was considered a top fighter pilot in his squadron and a true hero. When his Spitfire was hit by German fire close to the ground, instead of bailing out he revved the engine in order to avoid crashing into the village and killing civilians. The burning plane crashed into a nearby field; when found, its dead pilot was still in the cockpit. That same month, on the safer side of the Atlantic, my grandfather published the first five volumes of *The Dictionary of American History*, to be completed by year-end.

October brought forth a blaze of three books: a third Pulitzer Prize winner for Sherwood with his play *There Shall Be No Night*; *John D. Rockefeller: The Heroic Age of American Enterprise*, the two-volume Scribner debut for prolific historian and biographer Allan Nevins, who was to author some fifty books in all; and finally, eclipsing all competition, Hemingway's most successful instant bestseller, *For Whom the Bell Tolls*. Published just after the conclusion of the Spanish Civil War, it represents the fruits of his own wartime experiences (like *A Farewell to Arms*, a decade earlier) and remains one of his most beloved novels. Considered too racy at the time by the censors in the US Post Office, it was declared "unmailable." (Today it could be taught in high school.) It too was made into a memorable film—this time in color— again starring his good friend Gary Cooper, now alongside Ingrid Bergman. The film was nominated for nine Academy Awards, including Best Picture, Best Actor, and Best Actress. Hemingway was again on top.

The month after the book's publication, he also had a new wife, his third, Martha Gellhorn, a fellow and equally talented journalist. They had met while covering the Spanish Civil War. He bought a villa in Cuba, the Finca Vigía (Lookout Farm), his home for the next two decades and now a museum. His publisher—always accompanied by my grandmother, she stressed to me—visited him there and became especially fond of Martha, whose novel *The Heart of Another* (1941) my grandfather published, followed three years later by *Liana*. (My grandmother, I should add, was equally fond of Martha.) It caused some friction in the friendship between Scribner and Hemingway, who wanted his wife listed as "Martha Hemingway" on the cover. She had other ideas. My grandfather sided with Martha. But the friendship and publishing partnership survived Hemingway's jealousy over his wife's independent—and considerable—literary achievements as a first-class journalist and author in her own right. Their marriage, alas, would not. The new war in Europe would soon lure her back as an intrepid correspondent. Hemingway wrote to her, "Are you a war correspondent or a wife in my bed?" When the answer was clear, not to be left behind, he would follow—on separate paths.

CHAPTER 9

The Pen and the Sword

A MONTH BEFORE THE ATTACK ON PEARL HARBOR BROUGHT America into the war, my grandfather published Scott Fitzgerald's last and unfinished novel, *The Last Tycoon*. He had written to Scott in Hollywood about the novel-in-progress four years after *Tender Is the Night*. As a young editor, I came upon that letter while researching Fitzgerald in our Princeton archives. It was touching, encouraging, and prophetic. Scribner was thrilled by the author's news. No one, he stressed, could better write a novel about the movie business than Scott, who had been earning his living out there as a screenwriter for MGM—indeed a lucrative living, despite the fact that his scripts rarely saw their way onto the screen. The sad fact is that his hefty annual salary (close to a million in after-tax buying power today, with which he supported Zelda in a sanitarium and their daughter, Scottie, at boarding school) was squandered on drinking and entertaining, leaving the author often on the verge of bankruptcy. But Scott, now sober and hard at work on the novel he expected to revive his critical and financial fortunes, would die before finishing it. His contemporary, friend, and fellow Scribner author Edmund Wilson came to the rescue.

Wilson edited the novel (including the author's fascinating notes for its completion) and Scribners published it in a volume, together with *The Great Gatsby* and a few of his best short stories, in November 1941. The *New York Times* reviewer J. Donald Adams called it "the best piece of writing about . . . Hollywood and the movies." He concluded, "Fitzgerald's career is a tragic story, but the end is better than it might have been. And I think he will be remembered in his generation," a magnificent prediction—and understatement. Unfortunately my grandfather and Max Perkins had felt compelled to turn down Wilson's next book, a brilliant collection of essays on writers and writing, *The Wound and the Bow*. As much as they admired Wilson, there was an insurmountable problem: Wilson included a chapter on Hemingway in which he speculated about that macho author's insecurity about his masculinity. That would have broken Scribners' relationship with their most famous author; in fact, Hemingway wanted to kill Wilson when the book was published—but, fortunately, not by us. We escaped the fallout.

The next year, 1942, saw a new Rawlings book—her memoir, *Cross Creek*—hit the bestseller list, followed by her close friend and confidante Marcia Davenport's rich family saga about the steel mills in Pittsburgh: *The Valley of Decision*, the year's number-two bestseller. An "Upstairs/Downstairs" in the household of a wealthy mill owner, it was a literally riveting story of a young Irish housemaid, Mary Rafferty, who falls in love with her boss's only son, Paul. Her family, all workers in the mill, go on strike, violence is threatened, and that's all I need disclose about this gripping tale woven into a tapestry of American steelmaking and social history. The author of *Mozart* never skimped on research, and she never tempered her passion for her subjects. Marcia was richly rewarded: The film rights sold for a million dollars in today's currency. Three years later, that film, starring Gregory Peck and Greer Garson, would be the top-grossing movie of the year and gain Garson her sixth Oscar nomination. From then on, all of Marcia Davenport's novels would become bestsellers.

Marcia was devoted to her editor Max Perkins. Decades later, when I visited her on the West Coast, I spotted his large portrait photo in a silver frame behind her desk. When I reissued our volume of letters between Perkins and his authors, *Editor to Author*, in the late 1970s following Scott Berg's celebrated biography, she was the obvious author to write the introduction. But I must share two stories that shed new light on their relationship. The first, from my father, I could never print while Marcia was alive (she died in 1996). It reveals the "passive" side of Perkins's editorial technique—and genius. The second is from Marcia herself.

One day Marcia, her partial manuscript in hand, came in to see Max. She was agonizing aloud, sharing her torments of the damned: How was she ever going to get the book written and how was she going to develop her characters?—and so forth. Perkins sat attentively "taking notes"—doodling pictures of Napoleon, as was his habit. With his hearing aid now turned off, he was almost stone deaf; he heard virtually nothing of the author's impassioned monologue. He just sat there the whole time nodding and mumbling encouraging words and doodling until finally, after about an hour, the troubled author stood up, heaved a great sigh of relief, and said, "Max, I can't tell you how helpful you have been. Your advice is *infallible*."

Another time, several years later and not long before his death, Marcia said to him, "Max, if anything happened to you I don't think I could ever write another book." He replied, "In that case, I have failed you." He did not. Marcia would go on to write three more novels, all bestsellers, and a celebrated autobiography after her indispensable editor's death.

On a more martial note, 1942 saw the first of the three-volume set *Lee's Lieutenants* by the general's Pulitzer Prize–winning biographer Douglas Southall Freeman. Completed in 1944, it would remain his most popular work, still in print today. The Roman poet Horace wrote that his books would remain "more lasting than bronze." The statues of Lee may be removed from our public squares, as now seems to be their fate, but Freeman's books will last. A new one-volume abridgment was published by Scribners in 2001.

In February 1943 my father graduated from Princeton several months early and at the top of his class, the first *summa* in the family. During the war years graduation was accelerated to provide new officers for the armed services. He had already been recruited out of the classics department to use his skills at Greek and Latin—as well as his proficiency in French, German, and mathematics—at cracking enemy codes. As class salutatorian he delivered his speech in Latin, as was—and remains—the Princeton custom. My grandmother, not aware that the senior class had all been given English translations and cues for clapping, groaning, and laughing, was amazed that all the students seemed to understand Latin. To her, it was all Greek.

I am not inclined to write hagiography, but I must note here that my father was one of the top students in Princeton's history. The recruiter knew his mark. So although he would have preferred to serve on a ship in the Pacific, the new ensign was sent to Washington to be a cryptanalyst in the Navy's OP-20-G group, which received intercepted Japanese signals and went to work deciphering them. They succeeded in spades, breaking JN-25, the chief naval code, and advancing our victory in the Pacific. For years my mother and I had no idea of what he did during the war; it was all classified until the 1980s and he never confided a word. He was as silent as his uniform in the cedar closet, kept fresh because he was still in the reserves. We knew only his rank, lieutenant. When it was all finally declassified and he shared his story, I asked my father why the Japanese didn't come up with tougher codes as we were sinking their supply ships right and left. He replied that they didn't consider a race so inferior to theirs capable of breaking them. My elder son—a schoolboy at the time—commented, "So much for theories of racial superiority."

A few months after my father's departure for Washington, another major reference work was published: the *Atlas of American History*, again with James Truslow Adams as editor-in-chief, this time presiding over a team of sixty-four distinguished contributing historians. In November my grandparents attended the launching of the Victory ship *Charles Scribner*, named in memory of CS II and christened by my grandmother with a bottle of champagne broken over the bow. I still treasure its mahogany case with silver plaque for preserving family keepsakes.

By the beginning of 1945, as the nation prepared for victories in Europe and the Pacific, Scribners was preparing to celebrate its centennial the next year. Biographer Roger Burlingame, son of our famous editor Edward Burlingame, had been commissioned to write the official history of the firm for that anniversary, *Of Making Many Books: A Hundred Years of Reading, Writing, and Publishing*.

At the same time, Scribners announced a prize in American history—a hefty one in today's dollars, approaching $200,000—for "the most important and interesting book-length manuscript on any phase of American history from the discovery of America to the present day." It was won by Allan Nevins for his monumental history of the Civil War, *Ordeal of the Union*, eight volumes in all, published between 1947 and 1971.

Just in time for the firm's centennial celebration in October of 1946, my father, Charles Scribner IV, who was then and thereafter known as Charles Scribner Jr. (to the confusion of bibliographers and Internet listings), joined his father and company at 597 Fifth. If only his parents had not silently jettisoned his fleeting middle name, Hildreth—preserved only on his birth certificate—so much numerical redundancy could have been avoided. Truth be told, if he'd followed his heart, not his sense of filial duty, he would have returned to Princeton. He and Robert Goheen, a decade later Princeton's president, were among the first recruits to the new Woodrow Wilson Fellowship, set up to attract top students to return for graduate school and teaching. But he thought it would break his father's heart not to join the firm; by then my grandfather's health was already precarious (he would live only five more years).

> *My father never gave me, by fire or water, a baptism into publishing; he wasn't a baptizing type. I don't think he would have known what to say or do. He adopted the sink-or-swim method, so the first month I was at Scribners, my assignment was to deal with Ernest Hemingway on an illustrated edition of A Farewell to Arms. It was a good place to start, but in hindsight it seems incredible that I should have been entrusted with that job.*

As he explains in his memoir, *In the Company of Writers*, my father was immediately put in charge of advertising, as young Max Perkins had been by CS II. He had to do everything on the fly: write ad copy, jacket flaps, catalogs, you name it. His father and Max had given him the Hemingway assignment to insulate themselves from Papa's ire. The problem was simple: Hemingway hated the illustrations. Charles Jr. would have to take the heat as he was charged with asking the author to write an introduction to this new edition, aptly timed following the conclusion of a second world war. It contained a telling remark about his publisher, the man he called his "best friend." He wrote that my grandfather knew "a good deal about horses, as much as a man probably should be allowed to know about the publishing business, and, surprisingly, something about books." Hemingway thought of him not as a literary type, a man of letters, but as a horseman. This was key to their friendship between author and publisher; it explains why my grandfather was the only one in the house who could make suggestions to Hemingway without being rebuffed. He was also the only one who could persuade him to make changes, as he would do on the author's next novel, *Across the River and into the*

Trees, which originally contained some highly offensive passages describing the character based on Hemingway's ex-wife Martha. He would listen to his friend and fellow sportsman as he would never to a literary professional, editor, or author with whom he felt in constant competition.

On one occasion, Max had to appeal to my austere great-grandfather to restore (sans asterisks) some four letter words that had been sanitized in a Hemingway novel. CS II asked him what words were at stake. Max excused himself, repaired to his office, returned with a note, and handed it to him. "Max," he said, "you can't even say the words aloud to me and you expect me to publish them?" That was life at Scribners. By the time my dad arrived, Max's health was failing. The cause, as with his most famous writers Hemingway, Wolfe, and Fitzgerald, was too much drinking. My father was fond of Max and fully appreciated his superb editorial talents, yet he found him by this time somewhat "quirky" in his judgment about new books, especially in the realm of nonfiction, which Perkins treated as plainly inferior to fiction and, at this late stage, not worthy of the highest standards for acceptance. Once detecting my father's lack of enthusiasm for a new title, he lectured his young colleague, "You've got to learn to like the books we do." My father replied to himself, "Well, some-day I'll do the books I like."

That same year a young editor arrived from Macmillan (publisher of Margaret Mitchell) who would soon take the lead: Burroughs Mitchell, who was followed the next year by Harry Brague from Dodd, Mead (most famous as G. K. Chesterton's and Agatha Christie's publisher). The timing was fortuitous, for on June 17, 1947, Max died. I can't imagine how hard a blow that must have been to my grandfather. Three decades later I stumbled upon the telegram Hemingway sent that day to his publisher: "What awful luck. Deepest sympathy [to] you and all at Scribner. Have cabled Louise. Ernest." I was stunned, and briefly tempted to trash it as unworthy of Hemingway's legacy. He surely knew how devastated my grandfather was. "What awful luck"? But better instincts prevailed, and it has been preserved and published. Hemingway would more than compensate for that cursory cable within five years in the most moving letters to my grandmother and father upon the sudden death of his "best friend."

Perkins had lived to edit Marcia Davenport's next best-selling novel, *East Side, West Side*, published four months after his death in the same month, October, that launched a new science fiction writer for Scribners—Robert Heinlein with *Rocket Ship Galileo*. Perkins had also lived to read the manuscripts of two great novels that would later be edited by his younger colleagues: Alan Paton's *Cry, the Beloved Country* and James Jones's *From Here to Eternity*. Both first novels would become huge bestsellers and cap Perkins's legacy. Paton's novel, by an unknown schoolteacher in South Africa, dealt with the cruelty of racism in his native land that would be adopted as the national policy apartheid the year it was published, 1948. The manuscript, like Jones's, had come in over the transom, without an agent. The first to read and recognize its potential was a quixotic editor in his eighties named Charles Dunn, who sat outside Perkins's office and spent most of the day chewing tobacco. My father described him as a "non-acquiring editor." Evidently his fame as a Princeton pitcher in his youth explained his presence at Scribners over six decades. But his discovery of Paton was better than any shutout game. It was worth the wait.

The novel got off to a slow start—no one expected the classic bestseller it was destined to become—but it soon won rave reviews. My father wanted to run an ad of review quotations to highlight this achievement. Perhaps harking back to his study of Greek drama, he came up with an inspired headline: "A Spontaneous Chorus of Praise." He later claimed this coinage as his "single contribution to book advertising" and was pleased as punch when the Book-of-the-Month Club used it as their headline for its new main selection. As a third-former at St. Paul's almost twenty years later, I would write my first term paper on that novel (along with his collection of stories, which my dad retitled *Tales from a Troubled Land*, a vast improvement over Paton's original, *Debbie Go Home*). To my amazement, he sent my first draft to Paton, then under house arrest for his anti-apartheid writings, and then reported back to me that Paton had liked it but noted that I must have "a very old typewriter"—some of my spellings, never a strong suit, were Elizabethan.

That summer of '48, my father met at a dance in Morristown a dazzling girl named Joan Sunderland, who a year later would become his bride. Early in their courtship, she told me, he gave her a copy of *Cry, the Beloved Country*. The novel would melt any heart. Good choice. For my parents' wedding, Marjorie Rawlings sent a magnificent Audubon bird print—most appropriate from the author of the story collection *When the Whippoorwill* (1940). Hemingway, in turn, had offered in a letter to my grandfather an inscribed set of his books as a wedding gift. By some terrible oversight, the offer was never passed along to my father. Hemingway, having received no response, wrote back: "Think young Charlie makes a mistake not to have some of those aged books for doorstops." Worse still, my grandparents had failed to include Mary ("Mrs.") Hemingway on the invitation. But the friendship and publishing partnership survived this passing thunderstorm. His new novel, *Across the River and into the Trees*, the first in a decade, would be published the next September. If judged an inferior novel by most reviewers, it nonetheless was the bronze bestseller of the year.

My father liked to tell the story of how, on their honeymoon in Santa Barbara, my mother watched him unpack a pile of books and asked, with some concern, why he had brought them along. "That's my business," he replied. Then, seeing her expression, he quickly added, "I mean I'm in the book business." If 1951 looms large in my memory, it is not just because it's the year I was born. Several months earlier, in February, Scribners' rare book department had the greatest coup in its long history: the discovery and acquisition of the Shuckburgh copy of the Gutenberg Bible.

As part of its sale by David Randall, the head of our rare book department, to Arthur Houghton Jr., Scribners received several pages of an incomplete Gutenberg, one of which would "perfect" the incomplete copy owned by the General Theological Seminary downtown. Randall was thrilled since he now had a "page of great price." But he didn't reckon on my father, whose sister had married a professor at the seminary and lived there. Typical of Dad, he decided not to sell the page to General, but to make a gift of it. Randall's disappointment must have been exceeded only by bafflement. But that was my father. He always thought it was more blessed to give than to sell. And I've inherited his disinclination to be a collector of anything. Our family, much to everyone's surprise, owns no rare books. They have all been given away over the years—mostly to Princeton. Once again, as Fitzgerald said, "The victor belongs to the spoils." Who wants to be owned by such ephemeral possessions? The only things I've ever collected are mementos—and memories. They remain priceless.

That same month saw James Jones's first novel, *From Here to Eternity*, jump to number one on the bestseller list. Set in Hawaii in the months leading up to the attack on Pearl Harbor, this sprawling, earthy novel of army life made a tremendous splash, winning the National Book Award and being voted among the century's one hundred best novels by the Modern Library Board. Two years later it hit the bestseller list again with the release of the Academy Award–winning film starring Burt Lancaster, Montgomery Cliff, Deborah Kerr, Donna Reed, Ernest Borgnine, and Frank Sinatra. It revived Sinatra's Hollywood career and won him an Oscar. His star never dimmed thereafter. The novel would later enjoy two adaptations as a television miniseries and even a musical. Above all, it put Jones on the literary map, as well as his young Scribner editor Burroughs Mitchell, who did all the heavy lifting during those last few years of revising the manuscript with the fledgling author. In that, he served as a worthy successor to Perkins with Wolfe. Hemingway, on the other hand, was not impressed or pleased by all the adulation. "It's the end of writing," he wrote to my grandfather, referring to the author as "your Corporal Jones," the lowest insult he could coin. But the novel put Scribners back on top—for the time being.

The month I was born, May, saw—by divine coincidence—the publication of Cardinal Spellman's novel *The Foundling*, about a baby boy placed in the Nativity crèche at St. Patrick's Cathedral. It too hit the bestseller list. My father noted to me, after I became a Catholic, that the author had a large captive audience. Actually, Cardinal Spellman did not write it; he had a ghost writer—but that goes with the red hat. All the royalties were paid to the Foundling Hospital, which for several years was our next-door neighbor when we lived on East Sixty-Eighth Street with our firstborn son. Spellman and my grandfather enjoyed their drinks together, and he gave his publisher an inscribed photo portrait, which I later hung in my father's room at the Catholic nursing home where he died—I wanted to be sure the nuns and staff gave him special attention.

When I arrived on the scene, my grandfather slipped into my mother's hand an emerald ring, which I later gave to my daughter-in-law on the occasion of its encore. Having a son and namesake still counted a lot in our family. At my father's birth, thirty years earlier, my great-grandmother asked her son what the baby was. "The doctor says it's a boy," he replied. "You'd better go in and check. Doctors often get these things wrong." But my grandfather's joy was short-lived. Nine months later, he would die of a heart attack at the age of sixty-two.

My grandfather's death, if not a total surprise, came as a shock to my grandmother, who was waiting for him to come home from a doctor's visit before getting the call. He had suffered for years from an enlarged heart and an aneurysm of the aorta. It ruptured, and he died instantly. His funeral was packed; in fact, several hundreds more stood in the February cold outside the small Episcopal church where Ritchie and I would be married almost thirty years later. The overabundance of flowers spilled out and lined the pathway to the entrance. Hemingway could not get there in time from Cuba, but he sent the most memorable of condolence letters.

To my grandmother the distraught author wrote: "Now my dear and good friend is gone and there is no one to confide in nor trust nor make rough jokes with and I feel so terribly about Charlie being gone that I can't write anymore." A week later he mailed an equally heartfelt letter to my father, who was still on active duty as a naval lieutenant engaged once again in breaking enemy codes during the Korean War:

> *I won't try to write to you how much he meant to me as a friend and as a publisher. He was the best and closest friend that I had and it seems impossible that I will never have another letter from him. It does not do any good to talk about it and there is nothing to say that makes it any easier. Since he had to die at least he has gotten it over with. If there is anything practical I can do please let me know. . . . I will try and not worry you about finances nor about anything else. You don't have to write me letters nor have me on your mind in any way. I know what a terribly tough job you have now with Navy, Estate, and the House of Scribner to look after. They shouldn't do that to any human being. Please take it as easy as you can and feel free to call on me in any way that I can be of help. . . . This is not a good letter, Charlie. But I still feel too sad to write a good one.*
>
> *Your friend,*
> *Ernest Hemingway*

With typical Papa precision, he then added this postscript: "Am sorry I don't know your rank so address this as a civilian. EH"

My father later commented in his book of essays, *In the Web of Ideas: The Education of a Publisher*, that he could "not imagine a kinder expression of condolence or a more delicate assurance of loyalty. And in the lovely phrase of Dickens, he was better than his word. For the next nine years of his life, he was as easy to work with as any author I have ever known."

CHAPTER 10

A Scholar Steps Up

AFTER SEVERAL MONTHS OF TRAVELING ONE DAY EACH WEEK TO New York to the Scribner offices, my father was finally relieved of his Navy duty in Washington and by summer we were living with my grandmother at Dew Hollow in Far Hills. She remained isolated and inconsolable; my father was commuting, as his had done, each day back and forth to the city. My mother had only a one-year-old for company on two hundred acres of hunt country. At summer's end, we moved to the first home I can recall: my late great-grandmother Scribner's apartment on Madison and Seventy-Ninth Street, which her son had given to my parents as a wedding present.

At the office, as at home, my father had taken over his grandfather's desk. He found that in the twenty years his father had used it, he never moved anything in the drawers. He only made a small space in front for his cigarette filters and matches. That, to Dad, was emblematic of the state of the publishing firm. Nothing important had really been changed since his grandfather's day. No one was fired; it was a house of retainers. But at age thirty, he felt disinclined to shake things up. His colleagues, in turn, viewed him as a youngster. However brilliant, he was by nature polite and deferential to his elders. It is telling that the religion editor took it upon himself years later to drop eminent theologian Reinhold

Niebuhr (author of the "Serenity Prayer") as the religious books consultant without conferring with my father. He found out long after the fact; Niebuhr was too polite to complain—or even raise the question. Fortunately he remained our author, arguably the most distinguished on a most distinguished list.

My dad later regretted that he passed up a golden opportunity to hire one of the most talented editors around, Robert Giroux, not long after he took over. Giroux had invited my parents to the Met Opera, and at dinner in the Opera Club he inquired whether there might be an opening at Scribners for the post that Max Perkins had held. My dad was excited and sorely tempted, but he couldn't bring himself to upset Burroughs Mitchell and Harry Brague by putting a new editor over them; they both had been hired by his father only a few years earlier and took over after Max's death. Giroux instead went to work for Farrar and Straus and soon became a partner in that prestigious house Farrar, Straus and Giroux. It was a missed opportunity comparable to his grandfather's failing to promote and retain Frank Nelson Doubleday in the past century. I don't blame my father; I would have done the same—and regretted it as much.

In August, Scribners published Kurt Vonnegut's debut novel, *Player Piano*. A month later, Hemingway made the biggest splash of his career with *The Old Man and the Sea*, an instant bestseller that won him the 1953 Pulitzer Prize and was cited in his being awarded the Nobel Prize in Literature in 1954. He had dedicated it: "To Charlie Scribner and to Max Perkins." My grandfather didn't live to see the publication, but he had read the galley proofs. In my father's personal copy (now at Princeton) the author inscribed his famous motto: *"D'abord il faut durer"* [First of all, one must endure]. My father later coined a two-word translation more economic than even Hemingway might have imagined: "First: last."

My grandfather and Hemingway had kept up a lively correspondence as intimate, colorful, and often outrageous as only two closest friends could maintain. Filled with teasing—what Hemingway called "joking rough"—their letters would surely be misunderstood by readers today, especially by literary scholars whose literalism exceeds their grasp of inside jokes. I once received an advance proof of an article from a scholar seeking my permission to quote from family letters; she was convinced she had found in those letters the "smoking gun" that my grandfather and Martha Gellhorn had had an affair. The proof? A postscript from Hemingway saying, "Martha sends her love, whatever that means." Later, a letter from my grandfather to Hemingway describing meeting Martha (by then the author's ex-wife of almost a decade) and her young adopted son at the airport and quoting Martha's jesting that "she doesn't blame either of us" for the fact that she never gave birth to a child of her own. I could not convince the scholar that these were jokes; the only way I could get her to remove her offensive and ridiculous conclusion was to threaten to close our archives to future scholars and have Princeton explain that it was all her doing. It worked.

My father, by contrast, made a deliberate choice not to follow his father's example in his letters to Hemingway, who was almost a generation older. He thought it would be presumptuous. Instead, he decided to walk a fine line between seeming aloof and too familiar. "I knew," he later explained, "that Hemingway loved professionalism, whether in a writer or a bullfighter. He admired people who had a trade and stuck to it. That decided me: I would be a professional publisher." But in those letters there are glimmers of wit and warmth. In one, my dad commented that at the age of eighteen months I had taken to pulling out all the books from the bottom shelves at home. Hemingway wrote back, "What young Charlie is doing is trying to remove all the dead wood from publishing; make a note of it for his biographers." On another occasion my father wrote that he was concerned that I was becoming too citified (I still am) since I thought that "country" was just the word for my grandmother's house. On still another, "My children don't think I'm very smart. But I told them how come if I'm as dumb as you think, that I'm making all the money for this family?" Hemingway wrote back, "That's what I'm going to tell my children."

He, in turn, teased his young publisher (a new vestryman at St. Bartholomew's), "Charlie, I've been reading the New Testament and can't put it down: I can't wait to see how it ends."

On the business front, my father was alarmed that all our best books had been sold to paperback reprinters and the Modern Library, published by Bennett Cerf at Random House, for paltry sums by Whitney Darrow, head of the trade department, for whom books and authors were little more than a necessary nuisance for the privilege of being in the printing and publishing business. Dad felt our copyrights had been sold for a bowl of porridge. He was determined to reclaim them. For example, the armed services edition of *Gatsby*, which had been sent free to our GIs in Europe at the end of the war, had gained an estimated million readers of a new generation and was immediately followed by cheap reprint paperbacks published by Bantam Books under license. After the 1949 film starring Alan Ladd, *The Great Gatsby* was gaining momentum. The Bantam "tie-in" paperback featured not only an ad for the film but a cover illustration with Gatsby-Ladd that gave away the ending. Yet Scribners had no part in it. So my father proceeded to cancel all those licenses as they expired and take back the books for Scribner hardcover reissues.

Hemingway, who was proud of being such a major part of the Modern Library, was disappointed to see those editions disappear, but my father had persuaded him that he could earn far greater royalties from Scribners directly. It would soon prove the right choice. After receiving the Nobel Prize, Hemingway wrote to him, "It would be impossible to have a sounder friend or advisor than you have been." When Cerf made a pass for Hemingway, trying to lure him to Random House—or at least back to the Modern Library—my father had to craft a deft letter in reply.

96

Hemingway admired the parry, "I'm glad the way you got through that minefield." His loyalty was, in my dad's phrase, "cast iron." He also gave his publisher three rules of life: "Don't do knife tricks. Don't wrestle with bears. And, most important, always do sober what you said you'd do when drunk. That will teach you to keep your mouth shut."

That I survived my baptism at St. Bartholomew's, two days after my second birthday, is something of a miracle. While everyone was focused on the font held by a huge marble angel—by the sculptor, James Redfern, of the Albert Memorial in London—this toddler wandered a few steps away; like Curious George, tugging at the cord of a large steel fan on a ledge, he was spotted just before bringing it down to crash on his head. My two godfathers were both vice presidents and key colleagues of my father's a few blocks south of the church: his first-cousin George Schieffelin, treasurer of Scribners, and Henry Roberts, head of all book production. Both had come to Scribners after St. Paul's and Princeton, a familiar path. But it was a book about a propeller, not a fan, that made news that year, 1953: Charles Lindbergh's *The Spirit of St. Louis*. A bestseller in nonfiction, it would win the Pulitzer for biography.

My father was later to recall Lindbergh as the fussiest author he ever had to deal with. Lindbergh would measure the spaces around punctuation marks; to him every detail on the page had as much significance "as if it were a moving part in his airplane." So dad was aghast to discover that in the first printing of the Book-of-the-Month-Club edition two entire pages had been rendered as gibberish by a typesetting error; it was so bad that he felt he had to call Lindbergh himself and brace for catastrophe. But the colonel just brushed it off, saying that the mistake would make that first printing all the more valuable. I wish I could recall, two years later during our summer in Darien, Connecticut, the dinner my young mother had to cook and serve for our most famous neighbors, Colonel and Mrs. Lindbergh. At the age of twenty-eight, she found it a daunting prospect to be entertaining the first man to fly across the Atlantic solo the very year she was born. She found him aloof, icy, impossible to talk to—he never said a word throughout dinner—but Anne Morrow Lindbergh was warm and delightful. That experience surely provided my mother instant training in entertaining authors, something she and my father would do with natural ease and grace for decades to come.

In 1955 my father announced his decision to close the Scribner Press, the printing plant on West Forty-Third Street. The Flagg-designed building was sold, printing was outsourced, and space was leased in New Jersey for shipping and billing. It could not have been an easy decision, but there was no choice. No publisher would later maintain such a plant in midtown Manhattan; the costs were prohibitive. But no employee was laid off; my father made sure that they all found new jobs. On a more positive side of keeping up with the times, he then gave the Fifth Avenue bookstore a thorough renovation: Flagg's magnificent interior—I would later dub it the Sistine Chapel of bookselling—was now visible from the street through the huge plate-glass display windows. Inside, he had a new Scribner Young Readers' Bookshop added to the departments. Not coincidentally, he had just reissued the twenty-six Scribner Illustrated Classics titles with new full-color jackets featuring those artists of the Brandywine School.

In the field of juvenile books, always close to his heart (with two sons at home under the age of five), Charles Jr. took a creative hand in the design of Marjorie Rawlings's sole illustrated children's book, *The Secret River*, about a little girl whose mother was a hairdresser. Rawlings had died two years earlier, and the child's race was not clear. Was she black or white? Dad decided to solve the problem with inspired ambiguity. The entire book was to be printed in black ink on brown paper. With no imputed color now, he considered it his "silent contribution to dissolving the color barriers in the 1950s."

The decade of the '50s would include its share of fiction best-sellers for us—from Morton Thompson's *Not as a Stranger*, the top-selling book of 1954, to Gerald Green's *The Last Angry Man* in 1956. Both featured doctors and both were made into memorable films, the former starring Robert Mitchum; the latter, Paul Muni, nominated for an Oscar in the role. When my grandmother got to the part when Green's main character, Dr. Sam Abelman, suffers a heart attack, she called her son at the office: "If anything happens to that doctor, I'll never speak to you again." But the star-studded Perkins years had left an unfortunate legacy. The editors were on the perpetual lookout for the new Hemingway or Wolfe to arrive—like Godot. Their attention was fixed on the fiction front, to the exclusion of other areas of publishing. To make matters worse, James Jones's second novel, *Some Came Running* (1957), was savaged by the critics. The *New York Times* called it "a fictional disaster, clumsily written, crudely repetitious . . . cheaply vulgar throughout" (a description that must have pleased Hemingway as much as it pained my father, who nonetheless silently concurred). Vincente Minnelli's film version a year later—stripped down to a script and starring Frank Sinatra, Dean Martin, and Shirley MacLaine—fared far better.

To restore some balance to our list (a balanced list is essential to a general publisher's survival), my father set out to cultivate fields of nonfiction: history, biography, even practical how-to books. His hire of the first female editor of adult books, Elinor Parker, who had been manager of the bookstore, would prove providential. He had seen firsthand in the Navy how women (Waves) were "as well qualified as men for any intellectual task," he later explained. His break with house tradition was to serve the company well. By the time I arrived, there were as many women editors as men; by the time I left, thirty years later, there were far more, and both the Scribner publisher and editor-in-chief were women.

In 1957, my father was elected president of the Princeton University Press (the year after its first director, Whitney Darrow, retired from Scribners after four decades). He was very fond of its current director, Herbert Bailey, another Princeton alumnus. He considered Herb a great publisher of the kind of books that he valued—and read—most: scholarly books. The Baileys and my parents got together often in Princeton in and out of the football stadium, and I recall visits to their house from earliest days of childhood. When my father retired from the board in 1981—the year he became a grandfather of the next Charles—I was elected to succeed him. Today I consider it my favorite "family" publishing house, as well as the most distinguished. But then, I've always preferred scholarship to fiction. I must share Herb's recollection of those years, for it captures my father's essence as a scholar-publisher better than any I can recall, or could compose:

> *He participated as a publisher but did not hesitate to become involved in the substance of learned publications. He was judicious in his opinions but impatient of those who pushed themselves forward, were intolerant, or shaded the edges of truth. His integrity was unshakeable: I can recall a meeting in which a particularly difficult matter was discussed, and Charlie broke the tension by saying, "You can always tell a moral question because it makes you feel so rotten."*

That last quotation, which I've recycled for years, recalls a similar comment he made at a meeting at his church, St. Bartholomew's. He was elected to its vestry in 1958 and later served as warden. After listening to long pious digressions from the business at hand, he interjected, "In my experience, actions matter more than feelings." Back to business.

The 1950s saw an explosion of paperbacks in publishing. My father, as noted earlier, was not a fan of these cheap reprint editions that were sold in supermarkets, airports, drugstores, and newsstands like magazines. In fact, they were distributed like magazines—and by the same companies—as unsold copies had their covers stripped off and returned for credit in lieu of the books themselves. (It was cheaper than shipping back copies for resale.) But he was part owner of one of the most booming paperback publishers, Bantam Books, which had been launched by the reprint company Grosset & Dunlap.

Back in 1944 when Chicago tycoon Marshall Field bought Simon & Schuster and Pocket Books, the other publishers' alarm that they would soon be facing an invasion of cheap reprints was met by Bennett Cerf, founder of Random House, who immediately put together a partnership with four other publishers to meet the challenge. One was my grandfather.

Together they bought the reprint house of Grosset & Dunlap and launched Bantam Books. "We're in it for the money," he told new hire John O'Connor, who had been lured from the World Book Encyclopedia to run the company. Cerf was speaking for himself, not my grandfather.

Fast forward fifteen years to 1959. My father had inherited this stake in the reprint company and served his term as chairman, a post that rotated among the five owners. He liked and admired his fellow owners (the heads of Little Brown, Harper's, Random House, and Book-of-the-Month Club), but he disliked some of their practices. His admiration for the booming of Bantam Books did not lessen his intrinsic disdain for paperbacks. He also was no fan of Grosset's imitating Scribners' distinguished series of biographies for children and competing with their new discount versions. But the final blow was when Grosset, without ever consulting him, printed abroad a cheap illustrated version of our classic *Peter Pan* to capitalize on the next television broadcast starring Mary Martin. My father considered their edition "in atrocious taste, as if aimed at the dime-store market." But there was a far greater reason for his alarm. Importing those books for sale in America would have jeopardized our US copyright to the book and the steady stream of royalties to the Hospital for Sick Children in London, to which Barrie had assigned all his *Peter Pan* earnings.

Ignoring these real concerns ("We're in it for the money"), O'Connor chastised my father for not being "a team player." That did it. Dad had enough. He wanted out. But in a rash display of goodwill toward his fellow publishers and partners he offered to sell back to them his share of the company for the same price—not even adjusted for postwar inflation—that his father had paid in 1944! They were delighted beyond all dreams. Bennett Cerf later called it the most gentlemanly and foolish act he'd ever witnessed. A year later, they took Grosset public and Scribners missed sharing in a profit more than ten times the original price—upward of fifty million dollars today. My father knew he'd made a mistake, but it was done. His colleagues presented him with a large sterling Tiffany tray, as beautiful as weighty, with an effusive tribute above their signatures. It was displayed prominently on the front hall table for the rest of his life. Years later, when I finally learned the sorry story behind it, I asked him how he could bear to look at it each day as he picked up his mail. "That's how tough I am," he replied with a wink.

But there is a happier—if equally ironic—sequel to my father's antipathy for paperbacks. For years he resisted suggestions that he publish some himself. He preferred hardcovers and once said, "Having a line of paperbacks is like keeping a pet cobra in your living room." But by this time he was yielding to pressure. First he agreed to have some "student paperback editions" of our classics sold to the school and college market. Then when book-stores complained that they were left out, he charged full speed ahead.

In early 1960, ten months after Dad received his silver tray, our new warehouse and shipping center opened in Totowa, New Jersey. I loved visiting it as a child with him—not so much for its acres of books, but for the vending machines and insulated room with a huge IBM computer. Those whirling tapes and keypunched cards were my first glimpse into the digital age. The timing was perfect, for that very same month, February, Scribners was launching its new line of quality paperback books, The Scribner Library. The first twenty-one titles appeared with a uniform graphic design for their covers—no flashy illustrations befitting comic books—and in a larger trim size (like hardcovers) and durable bindings. *The Great Gatsby* was "SL 1"; it has remained the number-one seller since 1960. Scribner Library paperbacks were so successful that for a while the *New York Times* suspended the new separate category of "Trade Paperbacks." Most of them were ours. My father's competitors in the business credited him with unprecedented foresight in so methodically over the years reclaiming from reprinters all those titles with which to launch his own line. He relished the irony. In business as in war, what counts is the result—not the motive. "Actions matter more than feelings."

That February, Scribners published my favorite of all novels by Marcia Davenport, her last: *The Constant Image*. Taken from Shakespeare's *Twelfth Night*, it is also my favorite Scribner title. I have lifted that title and recycled it more times than I can count: "the constant image of the creature that is beloved." She set her best-selling modern—and doomed—love affair in northern Italy, like so many operas she knew so well. By this time, she was living in a villa on Lake Como, so every detail rang true, pitch perfect. Aubrey Menen in the *Saturday Review* wrote that reading the novel was "as much an education as a five-year stay in the country itself." Isn't that the purpose of fiction? The ultimate "virtual reality"—no goggles needed? Menen called it "a book in the fine tradition of Henry James and Edith Wharton. But Mrs. Davenport knows her own mind better than James ever did, and she can, when she is at her best, write Edith Wharton's head off." Not a bad way to start a new decade.

Hemingway, by this time, was not faring well. He had suffered two almost fatal plane crashes in Africa six years earlier. (After the news of the first crash, my father was awakened by a phone call in the middle of the night from a *New York Times* reporter asking him for a comment on his famous author's death.) He never fully recovered from those severe concussions. More recently, from 1959 to 1960, he had traveled to Spain to cover the rivalry of bull-fighters Dominguín and his brother-in-law Ordóñez for a series of long articles published in *Life* magazine as "The Dangerous Summer." In 1960, following Fidel Castro's takeover, he had to leave his beloved Finca Vigía, his home for the past twenty years. The new Cuban government then seized it. He never recovered from that loss either. Years of Homeric drinking, on top of a family history of depression, compounded now by diabetes, left him a shell of his old self in my father's eyes when he visited him at an apartment Hemingway was renting at 1 East Sixty-Second Street.

My father walked up Fifth Avenue with his editor Harry Brague to visit Papa and discuss the two books he was finishing: the first, his "Paris Sketches" (published posthumously as *A Move-able Feast*) and *The Dangerous Summer*. Both were virtually complete, but the latter needed major cutting (*Life* had just published less than half of its seventy-five thousand words), and the former, the "Paris book," as he called it, needed only some final polishing. Which one, he asked, should be published first? My father said the Paris book. But then after returning to the office, Brague second-guessed that advice and urged him to call Hemingway to find out if he really wanted to do that.

Dad called and said that if Hemingway would prefer it the other way around, then it would be equally okay. Hemingway went "into a tailspin." He had wanted decisiveness, not uncertainty. It was a serious error, my father realized too late, but fortunately not a fatal one. On the next visit, Hemingway asked his publisher to take a small suitcase to the office and lock it in his filing cabinet. It contained his will; he said: "Don't lose it." (They both surely recalled the disaster of his first wife, Hadley, losing a suitcase full of his early manuscripts in a Paris train station.) "If

I lose it, I'll shoot myself," Dad replied. "That won't do me any good," Papa countered.

Later in life, my dad would recall: "I am bound to say that working with Hemingway was like being strapped in an electric chair. All the electrodes were always in place, and it would need just the flicking of a switch to ruin me. I might do something quite innocently that would be taken amiss and I would be in outer darkness forever. It was hard. It required constant diplomacy to keep everything smooth. I don't think it made me cowardly, but it made me nervous."

The next day, Hemingway arrived unannounced at his publisher's office; he needed to look up something in his valise, he explained. Dad knew immediately why he really came. He just wanted to make sure it was still there. After shuffling around the papers, he returned to my father's desk all smiles and sat down in his publisher's chair. Chairless for the first time in his office, my father turned to play host.

"Would you like some coffee?"

"Yes, please."

"With cream?"

"Yes."

"How much?"

"Just enough to change the color."

Hemingway then added precise directions to the secretary for pouring the cream. "Only Hemingway," my father later recalled of this last visit with his most famous author, "would have thought out a specific formula for this commonplace operation. It was a kind of summary of his approach to life—accuracy, simplicity, and style."

A year later, after a repeat visit to the Mayo Clinic for depression, where he was given a series of shock treatments and discharged prematurely (he tried to walk into the propeller of an idling plane), he flew back home to Ketchum and, a day and a half later, shot himself early in the morning while Mary slept upstairs. It was Sunday, July 2, 1961. He was sixty-one. I'll never forget hearing the news on the radio that morning as my brothers and I played ball on the lawn at our New Jersey summer home. It remains as vivid as that schoolroom two years later when the announcement came over the loudspeaker that President Kennedy had been shot.

That evening, I watched my father sit silently at the dining room table, writing in pencil on a yellow legal pad. It was his official tribute for the press release, with the time, 6:30 p.m., inscribed at the top of the page. I saw it again almost four decades later in a display case at Firestone Library in Princeton while I was with my mother at John Delaney's Hemingway Centennial exhibition, which I had sponsored in memory of my father in the fall of 1999:

> *The magnitude of Ernest Hemingway's achievement as a creative artist has been recognized during his lifetime, and surely generations to come will agree with the judgment of his contemporaries. His books will always speak for themselves and will live on for centuries in that life beyond life to which every writer aspires. Speaking for Charles Scribner's Sons, and also personally, I can say that quite apart from the great privilege of having published all his works, the friendship and loyalty of Mr. Hemingway over a period of more than three decades constitute one of the brightest chapters in our history.*

The next day, back at the office, my father called Hemingway's attorney, Alfred Rice, to say that he had his will in the filing cabinet. It was news to Rice. Hemingway had never mentioned writing a new will. He would be right over, he said. "We'll have to see what it says; we may have to destroy it." That set off a silent alarm. My father called his own lawyer, Horace Manges—of Weil, Gotshal & Manges—to come over at once. The two attorneys together took hold of the handwritten document as it emerged from the valise until Rice had read enough to exclaim, with relief, "He's left everything to Mary."

My father never mentioned the obvious to me—or anyone: Hemingway's "cast-iron" loyalty was matched by his trust in his young publisher, son of his "best friend." It was to him, not his own attorney, that he entrusted his last will. My father now had a new client, his most important.

CHAPTER 11

Post Papa

IF 1961 WAS A DARK SUMMER FOR SCRIBNERS, FALL PRESAGED A brighter new year with the publication of our star illustrator Marcia Brown's *Once a Mouse*, which would win the Caldecott Medal in 1962. (Her earlier *Stone Soup* remains to this day my favorite Scribner children's book, a timeless lesson in generating generosity from scratch.) In February the New York Community Trust certified Flagg's building at 597 Fifth as a "Landmark of New York." Inside, my father arranged for Mary Hemingway to have an office of her own in which to comb through and organize the piled boxes of Ernest's manuscripts and papers that had been sent up from Cuba in exchange for her agreeing to "sign over" ownership of the Finca to Castro's government. It would prove for Scribners and the Hemingway Estate a priceless trade. Those cartons of literary treasures, now preserved at the JFK Library in Boston, would yield several posthumous bestsellers.

While Mary was sorting out estate matters, my father and Harry Brague focused on the final editing of the "Paris book." The manuscript had originally been delivered to them more than a year earlier by his close friend and unofficial assistant-in-chief A. E. Hotchner, who later recalled that it was virtually ready for publication; it just needed some final edits that Hemingway (and the Scribner copyeditors) would have given it had he lived. My father and Brague undertook this minor surgery—small cuts in redundant passages, trimmings, polishing—with no additions whatsoever. (This would remain my father's editorial policy in all subsequent Hemingway posthumous publications.) No one—not Mary, not his publisher, not an editor—would ever "play Ernest."

But what about a title? Hemingway had tried to find one that rang true. In his list of some forty tries, none did. They ranged from "How It Was Then" to "The Paris Nobody Knows," "To Love and Write Well," "How Different It Was," and even "With Due Respect." But Hotchner came to the rescue when he suggested to Mary "A Moveable Feast," a phrase he recalled Hemingway using to describe Paris. She loved it, and the rest is literary history. Woody Allen's *Midnight in Paris*—the best and wittiest reincarnation of Fitzgerald and Hemingway on film—quotes the phrase twice.

The book, an instant bestseller when published in 1964, featured such ex-pat luminaries as Scott Fitzgerald, James Joyce, Ezra Pound, Ford Maddox Ford, John Dos Passos, Sylvia Beach, Gertrude Stein, and Alice B. Toklas. It remains the classic evocation of postwar Paris and for many, myself included, the author's most beloved book. Unfortunately, it is no longer published and sold as originally conceived by its author. In 2009, Hemingway's grandson Seán, with his uncle Patrick's blessing, undertook a reedited version based on Hemingway's earlier drafts and notes, which he reassembled into what he then titled "The Restored Edition." But it "restored" only what its author had discarded in earlier drafts, including unfinished sentences as well as those redundancies cleaned up by my father and Brague in the final polishing. Its new editor approached it with the eye of a classical archaeologist (he is a distinguished curator of Greek and Roman art at the Metropolitan Museum), not the ear of a writer. Both Hotchner and I wrote in immediate protest—independently—to the *New York Times*.

The first location of the Scribner publishing firm in New York City

The founder, Charles Scribner (1820–1870)

John Blair Scribner (1850–1879)

Charles Scribner II (1854–1930)

Arthur Hawley Scribner (1859–1932)

·VOL. I. Nº I.   JANUARY. 1887   PRICE 25 CENTS·

SCRIBNER'S MAGAZINE

JANUARY

PUBLISHED MONTHLY WITH ILLUSTRATIONS

·CHARLES SCRIBNER'S SONS NEW YORK·
·F. WARNE & Cº BEDFORD Sᵀ STRAND LONDON·

Stanford White's design for the cover of *Scribner's Magazine* (1887)

Ernest Flagg's Scribner Building at 115 Fifth Avenue, New York City (1895)

Maxfield Parrish's design for the Scribner Press colophon (1902)

Ernest Flagg's Scribner Printing Plant and Warehouse on West 43rd Street (1907)

Ernest Flagg's Princeton University Press, Scribner Building (1911)

Ernest Flagg's Scribner Building at 597 Fifth Avenue, New York City (1913), interior of bookstore

Legendary editor Maxwell Perkins (1884–1947)

Charles Scribner III (1890–1952) on *Moonshine*, oil painting by Alfred Grenfell Haigh

Francis Cugat's 1924 gouache painting (Princeton University Library) for the cover of *The Great Gatsby*

Charles Scribner Jr. (IV; 1921–1995) in naval uniform

Charles Scribner III (V; 1951–)

In my letter, I stressed that both Mary and my father personally knew the author, whom sadly his grandson never met. They also knew firsthand what he wanted for this book. I added that, while I was sure the new edition would be of passing interest to scholars and students, "there is no doubt in my mind that Hemingway would not approve of the deconstruction of his classic. . . . The original edition is most faithful to the author's perspective as he approached his end. But, above all, Hemingway cared about works of art, and that is what the original edition remains: it will endure." Alas, on that last point I was to be proved wrong in the marketplace—except for those lucky readers who still buy hardcovers or read electronic books via Kindle or Apple.

A few days later, Hotchner confirmed in his own letter that Hemingway had personally handed him the "completed" manuscript to deliver to my father. On a later visit with Hemingway at the Mayo Clinic a few months before the author's death, the one thing Hemingway was worried about was that it "needed a final sentence, which it did not," Hotchner recalled. He concluded, "The book was a serious work that Ernest finished with his usual intensity, and he certainly intended it for publication. What I read on the plane from Cuba was essentially what was published." He felt strongly that Hemingway had been ill-served:

Ernest was very protective of the words he wrote, words that gave the literary world a new style of writing. Surely he has the right to have these words protected against frivolous incursion, like this reworked volume that should be called "A Moveable Book." I hope the Authors Guild is paying attention.

Seven years later, in 2016, I attended a launch party at the *Paris Review* for Lesley Blume's superb book on the Paris of that Moveable Feast, *Everybody Behaves Badly: The True Story Behind Hemingway's Masterpiece* The Sun Also Rises. There I met Hemingway's former secretary and daughter-in-law Valerie

Hemingway, mother of Seán. When I asked her about the controversy over her son's new edition, she told me that he had never mentioned the project, much less consulted her. Did she agree with my view of the original? Yes, she replied, our original published version was what Hemingway wrote: "I typed it."

The year 1962 also saw debuts of two very different sorts: the more traditional genre (if not in his verse) was the avant-garde poet Robert Creeley's first collection of poems, *For Love*. He would go on to write seven more for Scribners over the next fifteen years. Then a totally unexpected bestseller, the first of many in a brand-new field, appeared on the list: a book on needlecraft signed up by Elinor Parker. When she first proposed to my father the English needlepoint expert Erica Wilson's *Crewel Embroidery*, he was at a loss for words. He had no idea what "crewel" referred to—it sounded like an Elizabethan punishment. But he deferred to Elinor, and he soon reaped the rewards of his faith in her. Almost overnight, Scribners became the leader in a new genre, needlecraft books. It was soon a major source of new books, all produced with the highest quality of photogravure printing, and all profitable. Soon other publishers followed suit, but we retained the lead for the next two decades. (Our first son, Charlie, would enjoy his brief modeling career for Erica—sporting a Babar bathrobe and a Peter Rabbit pullover—at the ripe age of one and a half for her 1983 bestseller, *Erica Wilson's Children's World*.) It confirmed my father's conviction that the future for Scribners lay in broadening its lists, reclaiming the diversity of nonfiction titles that proved so successful a century earlier.

Over the next two years my father would set up new departments in science books, history, and above all—his future "crown jewel"—reference books. Key to success in this branching out from the Perkins legacy was the arrival of the future head of business operations, Franklyn Lee Rodgers, in 1962. A recent graduate of the University of Pennsylvania, Lee was recruited and mentored by my father's cousin George Schieffelin. He would eventually rise to become treasurer and then president of the company, overseeing all its operations. The chief difference between Lee and his predecessors on the business side—Whitney Darrow, Uncle Arthur, and even my great-grandfather Charles II—was that he loved books and had instant rapport with authors and their editors. When in 1964 my father chose Jacek Galazka from the old "subscription department" to run his reference division, he had in place two new colleagues. By the time I arrived a decade later they had become a virtual triumvirate at the house. I never detected a scintilla of tension, much less conflict, among them; they made an ideal team to take the company forward.

The new reference department enjoyed similar serendipity with the arrival in late 1967 of editor and, after just a few months, editorial director Marshall De Bruhl, who would work closely with my father in publishing a series of multivolume works that would soon dominate the field, just as the *Dictionary of American Biography* had several decades earlier, and Lange's *Biblical Commentary* and the *Encyclopedia Britannica* had a century before. Dad's office was on the fifth floor, but he soon spent his favorite time on the seventh, in the reference department.

During his days as a cryptanalyst in Washington, when he could not take any work home since it was all classified, Charles Jr. read extensively in the field of the history of science. One of his favorite books was by Princeton professor Charles Gillispie, *The Edge of Objectivity*. He had long wanted to commission books in this area so dear to his heart and intellect, fueled by recent years as president of the Princeton University Press. Those meetings brought him into close contact with scholars, and he wanted to be their publisher too. But scholars, he soon learned, don't work by commission; they pursue their own chosen paths to publication. Then in 1963, in a "Eureka moment," as he later described it, Dad thought of a solution: Why not publish a multivolume reference work on the history of science based on the model of Scribners' *DAB*? He took his idea for the *Dictionary of Scientific Biography*

(*DSB*) to Professor Gillispie, his choice for its editor. Gillispie loved the idea, and soon had his own office at Scribners for the next decade and a half.

My father then approached the American Council of Learned Societies, which decades earlier had been Scribners' partner in publishing the *DAB*. They came on board. The National Science Foundation provided a subsidy for the enormous scholarly costs, the biggest publication grant ever made by that foundation and the National Endowment for the Humanities. Originally planned as four volumes, the project expanded into sixteen by the time of its completion in 1980. But unlike his forebears, my father was not just its publisher; as a would-be academic and scholar in the field (but for his accident of birth), he immersed himself in all the details.

Next, the publisher turned author—in an article on the origins of Einstein's Special Theory of Relativity: "Henri Poincaré and the Theory of Relativity." He was thrilled when it was published in the *American Journal of Physics* in 1964. He gave me a copy to read; I, all of thirteen, pretended to understand it. The Nobel physicist Eugene Wigner, who did understand it, pronounced it "thoroughly professional." The year before, in May 1963, the journal had published a briefer piece, his first, on a mistranslation of a passage in Einstein's original 1905 paper on relativity. One evening after dinner, in his library where he worked on not only manuscripts but also equations, he noticed a non sequitur in the standard English book on Einstein's theory. He went back to the German original and found that the translators had made an error—something no one in the field had noticed for almost three decades. Perhaps that contributed to his Eureka moment that year? I'll never know. But let Gillispie himself, in his own recollection, spare me the charge of burnishing my father's credentials:

Charlie really should have been a scholar. All his instincts were right for that. . . . Charlie participated throughout in the same manner of a colleague rather than a publisher. He attended monthly board meetings [of the DSB] concerned with collecting the scientists to be included and with planning editorial criteria and mode of treatment. After a year or more of canvassing colleagues throughout the world and loosing graduate students onto all the reference works, we thought we had a list of 5000+ articles well, if still provisional, established. It was Charlie who then noticed that Newton was not on the list!

On Christmas Day, after all the stockings had been opened, a large—very large—package arrived at our apartment. My parents unwrapped it and discovered a handsome, antique-looking high-back chair with a red velvet seat and a card from Cousin George. He always gave magnificent gifts, but this one was puzzling: a single hall chair? It looked expensive, something from Bloomingdales perhaps or W&J Sloane ("from rugs to riches," as Louis Auchincloss once quipped). The next day at the office my father thanked his cousin for the gift, politely enough but in a manner that made it clear to the giver that the gift had not been fully understood. "Did you read the plaque on the back?" asked George. "What plaque?" Dad replied. "You'd better take a look when you get home." He did. On the back of the chair was a small brass plaque giving the provenance: its original owner was . . . Sir Isaac Newton! It remained my father's most cherished possession for the rest of his life. In 2019 I took it down to Princeton and donated it to the University Library, as the new librarian had just come over from Newton's university, Cambridge. No future generation will send it to Goodwill by a similar oversight.

During the preparation of the *DSB* my father also played author again, contributing to several of the biographies. He even rewrote (anonymously) the section on Einstein's theory of relativity when he found the professional version less than clear. He was uniquely qualified. He had recently, for recreation, spent several evenings after dinner retracing Einstein's equations in his study, but he hit an impasse: they didn't work. He went over them again and again until he found the reason: the publisher had misprinted a plus sign as a minus. (Small wonder that my mother would give him the family checkbook to recheck when the balance was off by a few pennies. He'd find the error in an instant.) As Einstein also said, "If you can't explain something simply, you don't understand it well enough." My father's love of science was based in art—the art of economy, simplicity. No scientific theory can claim absolute truth; the best ones are those that explain the most with the least.

From the beginning, CS Jr., who earned his degree in classics and, more broadly, the humanities, conceived of the *DSB* as a *humanistic* reference work comprising full-length essays in lieu of capsule sketches. He believed that "there are important advantages in an article that has a beginning, a middle, and an end and that attempts to present the material in its greatest simplicity":

> *Articles written in the tradition of the humanist—that is, as literature to be read and enjoyed—supply something very different from the flat, toneless inventory of facts that is touted as easy for retrieval from compact discs hooked to a computer. . . . We are concerned with imparting knowledge, not simply with storing information in a package. The former we want to store in human minds.*

The bright horizon of reference books in 1965, was for my father—but not his editorial colleagues on the fifth floor—hardly clouded by the passing of James Jones to a rival house. He had temporarily redeemed his reputation with the publication of his novella *The Pistol* in 1959 and, better yet, *The Thin Red Line* in 1962. Its reviews were far more positive than for *Some Came Running*, five years earlier. But in my dad's view, "His fiction was turning slovenly and scatological with little else to sustain interest."

Burroughs Mitchell and his editorial colleagues worshipped at the altar of Jones—but not my dad, who disliked his "bizarre behavior" as much as his prose. Once, he recalled, Jones "came into the office wearing dark-colored motorcycle goggles that covered half his face, spoke outrageous French, and boasted of taking a pulpit from a French church and turning it into a bar." That was enough for the warden of St. Bartholomew's.

When rival publisher Delacorte, who had been selling Jones's novels in their Dell mass-market paperbacks, made a huge offer (ten million dollars today) for his next novel, *Go to the Widow Maker*, plus the next two yet-to-be-written books, Dad decided to take a pass. He would not match it; he had read the manuscript. His colleagues were devastated, but he was relieved that he didn't have to publish it. When the *New York Times* reporter called him to ask how he felt about his famous author being lured away by a rival house, Dad replied, "My disappointment is under control." I've recycled that ambiguous coinage more times than I can count. It was taken as stoic grace; we at home knew better.

But the Götterdämmerung of the Perkins legacy came in the autumn of 1965 with the publication of the longest novel in our history, indeed one of the longest novels ever published in human history: *Miss MacIntosh, My Darling* by Marguerite Young. Perkins had signed up the novel in 1945; it was supposed to take two years to write. The author finally turned in her manuscript to Perkins's successor, Burroughs Mitchell, nineteen years later. It was 3,449 pages long; the published book, a year later, was twelve hundred pages and required thirty-eight miles of computer tape to typeset. It caused quite a stir at its publication. I remember reading about its launch by Scribners just a few weeks after I had arrived at St. Paul's. I knew nothing about book publicity, but I knew that hiring a bus (the novel's central motif) to take the literary press around New York City with the author was as unusual as the page count. It was an instant cult classic, but how many readers actually finished it?

The author herself described this tidal wave of prose as "an exploration of the illusions, hallucinations, errors of judgment in individual lives, the central scene of the novel being an opium addict's paradise." To Anaïs Nin, an early fan, it was "a search for reality through a maze of illusions and fantasy and dreams, ultimately asserting in the words of Calderon: 'Life is a dream.'" Is that clear? The dust jacket claimed—and the author later confirmed—that "at one time in the Gare Saint-Lazare in Paris, seven suitcases of the manuscript were lost—but were retrieved by seven men from Cook's with seven wheelbarrows." (Hemingway alas had had no such luck with his lost valise.) Kurt Vonnegut hailed the author as a "genius." Jerzy Kosinski called it "a massive achievement." Others likened it to *Moby Dick* and *Ulysses.* But forty years later, in the author's obituary, the *New York Times* labeled it "one of the most widely unread books ever acclaimed."

But *Miss MacIntosh* was not my only connection to our most famous editor that fall. The first day of school, as I was struggling with the padlock to my new locker in the gym, an imposing sixth-former (senior), whose locker was next to mine, lent a hand and then introduced himself: "Perry King." The name meant nothing to me, but then he added: "Our grandfathers worked together." What was his name? "Max Perkins." Perry was not only a varsity oarsman out of central casting, but also the lead actor in school productions. He would go on to have a long Hollywood career. He never played his grandfather on the screen (he looked just like him), but he did star as Max's most famous author in the 1976 television movie *The Hemingway Play*, to be followed a dozen years later by his starring in the Hemingway-inspired film *The Man Who Lived at the Ritz.* His grandfather, who had only daughters—five of them—would have smiled.

As a new student that year, one of my filial tasks was to bring a bag of recent Scribner books from my father to the school library. At the time, I assumed that he just wanted to save postage. In hindsight I suspect that it was his clever way of making sure

I got to know that library, designed by his Uncle Ernest, and the books inside. It worked. I formed a fast bond with the librarian Ann Locke, who soon became "den mother" to me and so many others at that all-boys school in the woods of New Hampshire. On my first such errand, after our 1965 Thanksgiving holiday, I recall *Miss MacIntosh* as the heaviest tome in the shopping bag for Miss Locke. The next time I saw the book was in William Hurt's suitcase in the 1988 film *The Accidental Tourist*, based on Anne Tyler's award-winning 1985 novel. The author evidently turned to read passages of *Miss MacIntosh* every time she faced writer's block. It worked.

The next year I took another book to the library, one that gained little attention at the time of its American publication (four year after its English debut at Faber & Faber), by a new Scribner author who would later loom large in the happiest of memories: *Cover Her Face*, the first novel by P. D. James. Over the next decade and a half—and nine novels for Scribners—she would become our star bestseller, the new "Queen of Crime." Far more important, Phyllis would become our closest family friend among authors. That first novel, acquired by Harry Brague in London and published in May 1966, was followed the next year by two more: *A Mind to Murder* and *Unnatural Causes*. It would take another dozen years and six more titles before she broke out as the brightest star in her genre of crime fiction. My father, an early fan, would prove that patience and perseverance pay off. But that happy story was a decade away—and worth the wait.

That same month, my father was elected president of the American Book Publishers Council and awarded an honorary degree by Princeton, alongside the astronaut Charles "Pete" Conrad, who had traveled the longest time in outer space up to then, eight days. Dad, too, set his sights higher. In January of the new year, 1967, he donated all the company archives—letters, manuscripts, business and editorial records, journals, photographs and graphic art—to the Princeton University Library. There was no tax deduction for this extravagant donation today worth millions; it was just a gift, pure and simple, to his alma mater—and to future generations of scholars. Supplemented over the next half century with additional documents and files, it now numbers (at latest count) 1,492 boxes, 750 linear feet. It remains, together with the papers of Scott Fitzgerald, the most widely used treasure of the library's special collections.

With libraries and scholarship in the forefront of his mind, my father sought a new idea for his new reference department. Ideas more than bestsellers had always captured his imagination. As a navy cryptanalyst during my first months in Washington, he distracted himself at home by reading Philip Wiener's *Journal of the History of Ideas*, a pioneer in "interdisciplinary" study which, now commonplace in academe, was a novel approach at the time. (Twenty-five years later, my son Charles would be the first in the line of six to graduate with an interdisciplinary certificate—in environmental science—from Princeton.)

His father had published Wiener's first book for Scribners, *Leibniz Selections*, in 1951, followed two years later by *Readings in Philosophy of Science*, a subject close to Dad's heart. There is some doubt among scholars that Archimedes had his "Eureka" moment in the bath, but the bathtub was in fact the site of my dad's, though not on the subject of volume displacement in water. There in early 1967 he had his reference brainstorm: why not an encyclopedia on the history of ideas?

By April, plans were announced for that new venture: *The Dictionary of the History of Ideas*, with Philip Wiener as its editor. When the five-volume set, with articles ranging from "abstraction" to "zeitgeist," appeared seven years later I was a grad student at Princeton in art and archaeology. My father gave me the new set, and I turned at once to "iconography," my current focus in art history. Written by the preeminent Polish art historian Jan Bialostocki, whose name I recognized thanks to my Rembrandt and Baroque studies, it was brilliant beyond all expectations. That was all I needed to read. Dad had converted me to reference books as the pinnacle of publishing. I was never to work in that department, but I recognized its preeminence early on.

For the summer vacation following my first year at St. Paul's, my mother's brother, Uncle Ned, took me on my first visit abroad. He was researching a book on the English canon law jurist—how is that for arcane?—Sir Lewis Dibdin. (That slim book would finally be finished and published three decades later.) We spent most of the time in London—with trips to Cambridge and Oxford and a few days abroad in Amsterdam, Brussels, and Paris. But England was at once my adopted home, and staying with my young cousins at their country house in Hampshire while Uncle Ned dove into archives at the Lambeth Palace Library convinced me where I wanted to spend the next summer vacation—at Woodcott.

Before I left for England in June 1967, my father gave me his most recent bestseller to read—for instruction as much as entertainment: *By-Line: Ernest Hemingway*, a collection of the young writer's columns for the *Kansas City Star*, where he honed his craft as a budding journalist who was already revealing the future novelist within. The pieces were short, crisp, and thoroughly engaging. Half a century later, I can still recall where I read them and feel the shaking of that old Erie-Lackawanna railroad car from Far Hills to Hoboken, en route to New York. At eighteen, Hemingway was only a couple of years older than this reader when he began his apprenticeship as a journalist. The book hit the *New York Times* bestseller list and was translated into fourteen languages—surely a record for a collection of old newspaper columns. It would be followed eighteen years later by our publication of Hemingway's subsequent columns for the *Toronto Star*, *Dateline: Toronto* (1985).

A couple of weeks later, my dad wrote a letter to his most prolific and distinguished English author, C. P. Snow, whose *Strangers and Brothers*, a series written from the 1940s to its completion in 1970 with its eleventh novel, would gain him as much renown as his famous 1959 lecture "The Two Cultures" on the gulf between the humanities and sciences in academe and society at large. I had just read Snow's *Variety of Men*, a series of short biographical profiles, which my father had published that year. I had yet to read one of his novels, but that would soon be remedied after my visit.

In that introductory letter, which I found recently, my dad asked Snow whether his "English son" might come and pay a visit to him and Lady Snow (also a distinguished Scribner novelist under her own name, Pamela Hansford Johnson) in London. By the time I arrived in July, Snow's reply was waiting for me there. My cousins were as amused as I was puzzled by the fact that under his signature, a very neat "Snow," his typist had added (in parentheses and all uppercase letters) "LORD SNOW." He was obviously very pleased with his life peerage recently bestowed by the Queen at the behest of his fellow Labour colleague, Prime Minister Harold Wilson.

I did follow through and visit the Snows at their townhouse on Cromwell Road, where I met their son, Philip, who was a fellow student with my cousin Jonathan at that most un-Labourite school, Eton College. Philip was so skilled in the classics, Latin and Greek, which I was then trying to master at the behest of my father, that I felt like a latter-day Tom Sawyer coming over from the colonies for tea. But to my surprise I later discovered among my father's papers, shortly after he died in 1995, a letter from Lord Snow about the visit. It was most complimentary, though with a bemused observation by the novelist that had he not known my father he would have assumed I was just another English boy. It wasn't an act, at least not a conscious one; during that perfect summer at Woodcott I simply became what I wanted to be.

Before that English summer I had concocted a fantasy future beyond St. Paul's: I would apply to Eton for a postgraduate year and from there proceed to Cambridge (the real one) for my university years. But that plan was soon undermined, upon return, by my deepening roots in Far Hills, a result of our new cottage there and a new horse, "Mischief" (from one of my lines as Cassius in St. Paul's production of Shakespeare's *Julius Caesar* that past academic year: "Mischief, thou art afoot, take thou what course thou willst"). Alas, Mischief lived up to his name on the field. Fox-hunting became the central event of my weekly schedule as I prepared to return to New Hampshire for another year at school. My grandfather would have approved; my grandmother decidedly did; my parents remained bemused. A second tie to these shores was a "Carnaby Street" dance party given by the lovely Markoe sisters in their large Tudor house a mile up the road from ours; it had originally belonged to my mother's Uncle Thorn. There I got to know better and better those two swinging sisters. A dozen years later the older sister, Andrée, would become my sister-in-law; the younger, Ritchie, my wife.

Back at school, my father sent me Lord Snow's novel *The Masters*, one of the best novels ever written about brutal if subtle English academic politics. It was set at Cambridge. Princeton, down the road, was soon looking far more inviting. The new year, 1968, would prove tumultuous for America—with political campaigns, two assassinations (Martin Luther King Jr. and Robert Kennedy) and riots. Closer to home, my father's key editor and link to his English authors, Harry Brague, died in March. I recall Dad having to fly back and forth from our Florida vacation to New York for the funeral. I didn't realize what a loss it was for my father until he invited me to accompany him to London that coming summer in order to entertain his list of English authors and reassure them that he would take them in hand personally and that he wanted to keep them at Scribners. They would have new editors, but their publisher would remain constant.

Before flying to London, I made a side tour with my mother to Princeton for an "admissions visit." While the student guide, Corbin Miller, a very poised sophomore who would later become a close friend and mentor, conducted his official tour, my mother gave me a simultaneous one in hushed counterpoint as she pointed out all the landmarks of her many dates there as a Bryn Mawr student. My college fate was by now a foregone conclusion.

In London, my father and I shared a room at the Hyde Park Hotel in Knightsbridge; most breakfasts, lunches, and dinners were spent "in the company of writers" (the apt title of his eventual publishing memoir). The names are now a blur—with two shining exceptions: the Snows, whom I already knew, and the most engaging writer I'd ever meet in my life: Phyllis White, better known as P. D. James. She, my dad, and I clicked at once at dinner at the Hyde Park Grill. I can almost recall what I ate—almost. She was as gripping in conversation as in her murder mysteries; I adored her. We would next meet seven years later on the other side of the Atlantic, my first year working at the family house. But that lay far off. I still had another year of school, then college, and then grad school before I could call myself an apprentice.

That fall of 1968, Scribners published the Pulitzer Prize–winning book by famous microbiologist René Dubos: *So Human an Animal*. The former professor at Harvard Medical School, now the eminent scientist at The Rockefeller University, had first appeared on the Scribner list with his 1960 biography of Louis Pasteur. Dubos was not only a towering figure in medicine specializing in "natural antibiotics" but also an environmental pioneer who coined the maxim "think globally, act locally." Both my father and my conservationist son Charlie would find him equally inspiring. He also embodied the kind of writer Dad had long wished to publish in this post-Perkins, post-Papa era.

In the following spring, my last at St. Paul's, Scribners published the monumental biography of our most famous novelist: *Ernest Hemingway: A Life Story* by Carlos Baker. He was selected by my father and Mary Hemingway to undertake this herculean task with access to all Hemingway's letters and personal papers. Authorized yet objective, it remains a half century later the standard work on the author—unsurpassed by the spate of scholarly biographies, psychobiographies, and pop biographies that have appeared (and disappeared) on bookstore shelves in the interim. Baker based his book on the *facts* of the author's life, not interpretations. It is the touchstone for all future scholars. When asked to write an introduction to its silver anniversary edition in 1994, I confessed that it also held a special place in my memory since its publication happened to coincide with my acceptance to Princeton for the next fall—an event no St. Paul's sixth former ever forgets.

That April—not always Eliot's "cruelest month"—I got a surprise letter from our former guide, Corbin Miller, explaining with utmost tact and powers of persuasion all the good reasons to accept Princeton's offer and not be tempted to forge an independent path elsewhere, unburdened by the weight of family tradition; this was, after all, the Woodstock year of 1969. Somewhat sheepishly, I wrote back that, yes, I would be going to Princeton in the fall; it was the only college to which I had applied. Originality was not yet a family tradition.

The summer after graduation, instead of heading back to England, I stayed on two months at St. Paul's as a member of a committee on the future of religion at the school—both in academics and in chapel. Little did I know then how great an impact that job—the first paid job in my life—would have both on my later college life and in religious publishing. There were twelve of us: four new graduates, four upcoming seniors, four clergy, and four lay faculty. When the report was submitted I found myself the author of a "minority report"—of one. No one joined in my recommendation that chapel services remain a requirement for students and faculty at the school; no one shared my traditionalist view that, once secularized, the school would never regain its identity as a church school. As I reread today what I wrote back then, I suspect it was already a foregone conclusion that within a year I would seek the solidity of the Rock of Peter as a Catholic. What I best remember from that night I played self-publisher and made copies of my report on the Rector's Xerox machine is that he was the one reader I sought to persuade—and I did. Chapel remains required at St. Paul's to this day.

At Princeton that fall I continued to follow my father's prescriptions for courses: Greek, English, history, and physics. For history I wrote my paper on the conflict between Galileo and the Church, based on a book Dad recommended but did not publish: Giorgio de Santillana's *The Crime of Galileo*. At the same time I was taking the hardest course in my life, introductory physics, leavened by some history of science as we traced the theories of the universe from Copernicus through Einstein's theory of relativity. Someone once said that taking physics at Princeton was like trying to take a drink from a firehose. But thanks to my father I got my first taste of science as a fine art, and its history as one of progressively beautiful—that is, clearer, simpler, more economical—explanations of the confusing, cluttered natural world around us. Three years later, for my senior thesis, it would prove invaluable in solving a problem of art history: the puzzle of reassembling a cycle of tapestries by Rubens. When asked by students, "What was the most important art course you took?" I reply, "Physics."

My father—my greatest teacher—would find his convictions in both science and publishing confirmed the next year with the first of several philosophical science books by a new Scribner author, Loren Eiseley. *Publisher's Weekly* dubbed this poetic anthropologist "the modern Thoreau." His first book for us, *The Invisible Pyramid*, published in response to the moon landing the year before, ponders inner and outer space, the vastness of the universe, and the fluid boundaries of human knowledge. "Man would not be man if his dreams did not exceed his grasp," he concluded. Two years later, it would be followed by *The Night Country*. One reviewer wrote, "Like the medievalists, Eiseley reads nature as the second book of God's revelation, mysterious and heavy with latent, lurking fertility." His publisher's faith in our new science book department was confirmed.

The fall season saw yet another Hemingway bestseller, his first posthumous novel, *Islands in the Stream*. Hemingway had left at his death a manuscript written from 1950 to 1951, a semi-autobiographical "sea trilogy" about a painter, Thomas Hudson, set in Bimini, Havana, and at sea. In it he drew from his own experiences fishing and later chasing German U-boats in the Gulf Stream off of Cuba during the war. My father, Mary, and Carlos Baker together edited it into a novel in "three acts." The title, coined to encompass the three, was my father's contribution—later made even more famous by the hit song recorded by Dolly Parton. As in *A Moveable Feast*, nothing was added to Hemingway's text; it was just a matter of editorial sculpting and polishing the largely finished manuscript. Many reviewers were critical in principle of such a posthumous publication, but in an unexpected twist Edmund Wilson, hardly a Scribner house herald, came to my father's defense in his review. The book was the year's number-three bestseller and was followed by the film starring George C. Scott as Hudson. It would retain a prominent place in the Hemingway canon for half a century. *"D'abord il faut durer."*

I was back at Princeton for my sophomore year when Hemingway's novel hit the news. A newly minted Catholic, I had signed up for a course in early Christian and medieval art taught by a young professor from the United Kingdom, Alan Borg, both to provide a cultural background to my adoptive church and to complement a course I was taking in Chaucer by D. W. Robertson, a legend in the English department in which (if not in classics) I expected to major. But by the spring term I was hooked on medieval art and iconography, that is to say, how to *read* images. (I soon discovered that reading images was much more fun than reading hundreds of pages of assigned books.) That term on weekends at home, my parents and I were glued to the television each Sunday evening to watch Kenneth Clark's *Civilisation*, a PBS series that would lure me for good into art history. It would also, a half century later, inspire my art book *Sacred Muse*, a religious offshoot of Lord Clark's highly personal survey.

By spring I had signed up for three art history courses—no English, no Latin, no Greek. My favorite course was again medieval: Early Christian and Medieval Architecture, also taught by Professor Alan Borg, who would eventually be named director of the Victoria and Albert Museum in London. That spring at my Catholic confirmation in Princeton I had as my sponsor, all thanks to my father, one of Princeton's most distinguished scientists and former deans, Sir Hugh Taylor—the only person to have been knighted both by the Queen and the Pope. Perhaps my father wanted to remind me that religion need not nudge aside science—that a devout Catholic had discovered the means of producing "heavy water," an essential component of the atom bomb.

If my father was disappointed by my choice in a major, he did not show it; in fact, he mentioned only that he wished he had taken more art history as a student. So I was off and running into a new discipline. I found few books to consult on the Scribner lists, except for Étienne Gilson's classics *Reason and Revelation in the Middle Ages* (1938) and *The Spirit of Mediaeval Philosophy* (1932). That spring some like-minded friends—led by Georgetown's future university professor and provost James O'Donnell—persuaded Professor Robert Fleming in the English department to create an interdisciplinary "humanities" course on the Middle Ages. He did, I took it, and it was such a success with students that it remained in the catalog and eventually grew into a formal Medieval Studies Program at Princeton, flourishing to this day.

But why am I digressing into the Dark Ages? Because in my burst of enthusiasm for these courses I told my father, already deep in new projects for his beloved reference department, that he should commission a *Dictionary of the Middle Ages*. Though I would soon "go for Baroque" in my choice of field, he did not brush off my suggestion. His motto was always "no rush, just do it immediately." He pursued the idea with Professor Joseph Strayer in the history department. A decade later, Scribners published the first—of thirteen!—volumes of the *Dictionary of the Middle Ages*, with Strayer as editor-in-chief. It would prove the most sumptuous of all his reference books, fully illustrated and with a color frontispiece at the beginning of each volume. I never proposed another reference project; I quit while I was ahead and went back to my studies.

The summer of 1971, before I took off on a month-long African photo safari with my grandmother Scribner I went to work as an apprentice in our Fifth Avenue bookstore. Perhaps the grand opening that spring of a branch bookstore in Colonial Williamsburg sparked the idea. I loved it all—the books, the camaraderie, the customers. A few years later my younger brother Blair would follow suit. I strove to provide Tiffany-worthy customer service, even delivering some books to a patient at Lenox Hill Hospital (a few blocks from our home). In hindsight it was excellent training for a future career upstairs in the editorial offices. Publishing books is theoretical until the sale is made and the book changes hands.

My one regret: I wish I knew at the time that my friendly and fun young colleague named Patti Smith would later be a famous punk-rock song writer, performer, and artist. I didn't realize who she was—or was to become—until my English cousin's wife Mary Pease gave me her book in London forty years later, *Just Kids*. In Patti's acceptance speech for her 2010 National Book Award, she confessed: "When I was a clerk at Scribner's bookstore, I always dreamed of writing a book of my own. When I had to unpack the winners of the National Book Awards and put them on the shelf, I used to wonder what it would feel like to win one."

A year later, my father hosted a grand publication party in the Fifth Avenue store for a book, but not one of his own. It was for Sir Rudolf Bing's *5000 Nights at the Opera* (a brilliant title with a nod to the Marx Brothers), published not by Scribners but by

Doubleday. A few years earlier my father had written to the general manager of the Metropolitan Opera asking him if he would consider writing his memoirs. My grandfather had published famous Met impresario Giulio Gatti-Casazza's *Memories of the Opera* forty years earlier; it is still in print. Sir Rudolf wrote back a very gracious letter explaining that he already had a contract with Doubleday (its publisher, John Sargent, was an avid opera goer), but then asked whether he might discuss some of its terms with him. My father was happy to oblige. Bing then began asking my parents to performances as his regular guests in the center box; performances plural because from the start it was clear to this high-strung general manager that they were the ideal guests to help him manage his official guests. My parents were always prompt, never questioned a direction, and were swift to follow his steps back and forth to the Grand Tier for refreshments during the intermissions (my mother, a professional figure skater, never hesitated; fast forward).

On one memorable night of the *5000*, the guest of honor was Maria Callas, the diva beyond all divas. She had had some cross moments with Sir Rudolf, who fired her at the peak of her career in 1958. She would return for two performances as Tosca seven years later, in 1965, her last at the Met. During the intermission, she announced that she would like a steak. When it was brought to the table she then complained that her knife was not sharp enough (Scarpia had an easier time with Tosca). Back in the box, seated for the next act, she was greeted by a spontaneous eruption of applause and cheers. La Callas turned to my father and asked with feigned innocence, "What should I do?" (She knew exactly what she should and would do but relished the dramatic pause.) "I think you should rise and acknowledge them, Madame Callas." And so she did.

My parents had for years taken an annual subscription for me, an avid opera fan. (I'd go to Italian and French operas with my mother, German with my father.) I was star-struck by their friendship with Bing, who was retiring that year, 1972. My father, never one to take generosity for granted, wanted to thank Sir Rudolf for all those invitations. So he offered to host the publication party in his store, itself worthy of a Zeffirelli set at the Met. Scribners had never launched a book by a rival publisher; the Doubleday folks were puzzled and unprepared as guests at their own book party. Sir Rudolf was pleased, and that was all that counted with my father. I just wish I could have been there. My own nights at the opera would come, but not for another five years.

The last term of my senior year in 1973 coincided with a new Scribner bestseller, *The Billion Dollar Sure Thing* by Paul Erdman, an economist and head of a Swiss bank who went to prison—a seventeenth-century Swiss dungeon (four star) in Basel—when the bank collapsed and he was charged with fraud. He was there for eight months—with fine wines and meals delivered at his expense—and wrote his first novel, which launched a new genre: the "financial thriller," in this case an elaborate international scheme to devalue the dollar for fraudulent gains. After posting and skipping bail he returned to America, was sentenced in absentia to nine years by the Swiss court, and declined to return to Switzerland. The novel, an instant bestseller, won an Edgar Award for the year's best mystery and was followed a year later by his next Scribner bestseller, *The Silver Bears*, about a Mafia-controlled Swiss bank, silver mines, and smugglers. It was made into an equally successful film (1978) starring Michael Caine, Cybill Shepherd, Martin Balsam—and Jay Leno! Erdman, like other best-selling authors launched by my father, would soon be lured away by a bigger house for bigger dollars, but it was a great ride. His next publisher, Simon & Schuster, would eventually own Scribners. All in the family.

The month I finished my Princeton senior thesis—on Rubens's *Triumph of the Eucharist* tapestries—our most distinguished Catholic author, Jacques Maritain, died. He had taught at Princeton and was elected professor emeritus (he called it his "Elysian Status") in 1956. Thereafter the Neo-Thomist philosopher was a local hero at the Aquinas Institute, our Catholic chaplaincy. In a flush of enthusiasm I mentioned to my dad that I'd heard rumors Maritain might be promoted for canonization. My father was ecumenical and a huge admirer of Maritain as an intellect and writer, but he considered him, from firsthand experience, no saint. "You be sure to let me know, Charlie, if it gains any traction. I'll send over all his author files to the Vatican and that will be the end of it." Maritain was evidently a charter member of the Difficult Authors Club. Once again, as my editor Michelle Rapkin cautioned me, avoid meeting authors you especially admire—especially *religious* authors, she added.

My final term at Princeton caught me in a dilemma: Where should I go next? I had applied to graduate school to pursue a PhD in art history, but only one: Princeton's. I didn't want to leave my adviser, the great Rubens scholar John Rupert Martin, or my Baroque studies under him. At the same time, I felt the tug of family tradition. Would I be the first of five to fail to move on to our house of authors? My father had counseled me, halfway through Princeton, to "do a favor to the person you will be twenty years from now." Those undergraduate years were not so much a matter of "higher education" (higher than what?) as a sound investment; those deposits of intellectual and cultural capital have paid rich dividends down to the present day.

When I got the news of my acceptance to Princeton for graduate school, I agonized over what to do. After days of indecision I mailed back the postcard with the box checked that I was declining the offer. Then I told Professor Martin that I needed to speak to him about my plans for the next year (when I would be working at Scribners). We walked into the art museum and sat on the first bench. As soon as he said that he hoped I would be continuing my studies with him in the fall, I knew I couldn't tell the truth—that I had already notified the dean that I wasn't coming back. I could not bring myself to decline this personal invitation face to face. I dashed off to Nassau Hall and explained to the secretary that I needed to retrieve the card I had mailed in, that I had "a terrible feeling I might have checked the wrong box." She found the card and, lo, my feeling was well founded—but easily corrected with a stroke of the pen.

That summer I was recruited by our local Auntie Mame, "Princess Pyne," to give an art history tour of Europe with the three belles of Holland Road—neighbors Holly Pyne and Andrée and Ritchie Markoe—the only European tour I've ever given. I'm glad I accepted her proposal; my sons should be equally glad. Six years later our foursome would regroup as two bridesmaids, a bride, and a groom. The next spring while I was immersed at Princeton in matters Baroque, our most famous novel hit the screens: *The Great Gatsby*, starring Robert Redford, Mia Farrow, and the incomparable (if far less known, pre–*Law & Order*) Sam Waterston. That film was itself Baroque. It featured a *style* more than a novel; the ads for fashion all touted the new yet retro "Gatsby style." Ralph Lauren got his big boost designing the costumes—pastel shirts and vanilla ice cream suits. The author's daughter, Scottie, mused in the press: "What next, white Gatsby teflon pots and pans?" If the film was less than a critical success, it did wonders for book sales. Never again would the novel sell fewer than 250,000 copies per year; it now tops half a million annually.

At the same time, my father was publishing the most lavish "art book" in our history (of not publishing art books): a large, coffee-table scrapbook of Scott and Zelda Fitzgerald, *The Romantic Egoists*. Culled from a huge collection of the author's scrapbooks now at Princeton, it presents the most vivid and immediate record of their meteoric rise in the Jazz Age they inspired, the original "beautiful people." At the publication party my parents hosted at our apartment, I got to meet both Scottie and her constant adviser and co-editor, Matthew J. Bruccoli. Both would loom large in our Fitzgerald future.

Not to be left out, Hemingway was given a weighty anthology by Scribners in partnership with the Book-of-the-Month Club: *The Enduring Hemingway*. My father made the selections for this nine-hundred-page collection of his best writing covering all themes—from early reportage to African hunting, war, bullfighting, and the sea. Dad's introduction remains, in this son's unbiased view, the best summary of the author's achievement. It also includes an original literary insight proposed by a publisher (imagine that): that in his early stories and his "stripping technique"—paring description to the barest essentials—Hemingway was influenced by James Joyce's "epiphanies" in *Dubliners*. Mary Hemingway wanted my father to remove that hypothesis; she did not want her late husband beholden to Joyce. But my father held his ground: Hemingway knew Joyce in Paris and was a fan. Art imitates art, not life.

The new year, 1975, was heralded by two major events in January: the publication of P. D. James's new mystery, *The Black Tower*, her sixth for Scribners. The good reviews and increasing sales encouraged my father to invite this delightful author to America for press interviews and a family visit. I remember so vividly her visit to my parents and grandmother Scribner in Far Hills. Granny was planning yet another safari—her tenth? (I've lost count.) Looking out her huge picture windows with vistas of Somerset Hills, the author commented, "I'd be happy just to sit here and enjoy the view." Less noticed at the time, but of far greater significance long term, Jacques Barzun arrived at 597 Fifth as my father's new "literary adviser." Barzun had just retired as provost of Columbia. My father didn't hesitate for a second; it would prove by far the greatest hire—indeed coup—of his publishing career. Jacques would become not only dad's key adviser and colleague on all matters literary and intellectual at the house but also my chief mentor—and editor—for art history writings.

On an impulse right after receiving my master's degree that June, and upon hearing my father say that he had lost an editor and was short a hand, I volunteered that I would like to move back to New York and help out at the office. And so, while pondering what my dissertation would be, I met Jacques the next week; he was already at his new desk. There was, quite simply, no university in the country that could offer a young scholar a more engaging, inspiring, or brilliant mentor than Jacques. He would set for me, throughout the next eighteen years, the highest standard for clear thinking and clear writing (the two are inseparable). My dad considered him "in a class with Dr. Johnson for encyclopedic knowledge, literary taste, and common sense." Cambridge University gave him the title, as an overseas member, of "Extraordinary Fellow." He gave it literal meaning. His editorial skills were so sharp that one Scribner author invented a new term for them: "Barzunizing." A new chapter was beginning for our house history.

CHAPTER 12

Professional Son

MY BOSS ON THE FIFTH AND EDITORIAL FLOOR WAS JACEK GALA-
zka, whom my father had moved from reference to run the adult
trade program. He sat in my dad's—and his father's and his
father's—old office. Dad had moved three floors upstairs (in fact
we took those stairs more often than waiting for an elevator—
much better exercise before gyms and health clubs proliferated
in midtown). He put a putting machine at the end of his long
new office to take his mind off publishing matters during breaks.
Down the hall was a large boardroom, where all meetings were
held, and at the other end of the floor, an executive suite for Lee
Rodgers and his business team.

On one of my first mornings arriving at the office with my
father—we walked together from the apartment when I was not
commuting from Princeton—I met an old lobby attendant, Sam.
He was a holdover from a previous generation when he ran the
manual elevator. It had long been automated; he now pushed the
call button. Sam greeted me as "Charlie" and my father more
heartily as "Charles." I alone detected a fleeting frown across
Dad's brow. He cheerily replied, "Hello, Sam." But I knew what
was left unsaid, perhaps out of deference to age. Several years
earlier, my dad and I had visited a Buick showroom in New Jersey. The effusive salesman, showing us model after model, kept

addressing my dad (whom he had never met) as "Charles." After the third or fourth time, my father replied in his most polite and courtly manner, "Please feel free to call me Mr. Scribner if it would make you feel more comfortable."

Jacek was the ideal boss: patient, kind, modest, helpful, and the hardest working person in the company. As a teenager in occupied Poland, he hiked across Europe and in England joined the Polish Armed Forces against the Nazis and was wounded in battle (something I learned only after his death in 2018). After the war, with a degree in economics from Edinburgh, he came to the United States and eventually chose a career in publishing. There was no aspect of the business he didn't know—and love. His enthusiasm was contagious, and he never failed to be positive in the most trying of circumstances (of which there was no shortage at this stage in general publishing for a private family firm up against giant corporations). My father once said that if he were in a foxhole under fire, he'd want Jacek beside him. His close colleague, Lee Rodgers, described him as "spirited, indefatigable, and selfless—words sometimes used too freely but not in this case." In short, I landed on the right floor that summer.

One of my tasks as the most junior member of the editorial department was to read and reply to unsolicited manuscripts that arrived over the transom. It wasn't time consuming; most revealed themselves as unpublishable by the first page. But in the back of my mind I remembered that Alan Paton's *Cry, the Beloved Country* had come in this way, and that kept me opening the packages. The most entertaining of the unsolicited manuscripts was delivered in person by an elderly blonde from Queens who arrived at the receptionist's desk once a year dressed all in white, from veil to shoes. I forget the title, but it was "dictated by God to Pope Pius XII." I dutifully left with the manuscript a personalized form letter, explaining that it was "rather too special for our general list." The Lady in White took it with grace—and returned the next year.

As I struggled to learn how to calculate profit-and-loss sheets for books under consideration, among other less glamorous tasks of assistant to the director, I decided to reward myself extravagantly for my modest paychecks: I wrote to Heim Gallery in London and said I wanted to buy the Bernini bronze crucifix I had seen there the previous summer, one of the series Bernini had designed for St. Peter's in Rome. I liquidated some savings— about the cost of a foreign sports car. I rationalized that the crucifix would last much longer, and arranged to have it shipped to the office. It arrived in a pine crate that looked like a small coffin, much to the bemusement of my editorial colleagues.

That fall, en route to my first Frankfurt Book Fair as Jacek's assistant—my first trip to Germany—I stopped off in Rome. It was a Holy Year. I went to St. Peter's to see the companion crucifixes and attended a pontifical Mass celebrated under Bernini's baldacchino by Cardinal Wright, a high-ranking American prelate. His young assistant (eventually the Cardinal Archbishop of Washington, DC) and I helped him afterward to his car—a Fiat, appropriately—each taking one arm of the old cardinal, who was a bit unsteady on his feet. At the last instant before leaving the basilica through a small side door, I looked up and realized that we were walking through the door (actually a false door) of Bernini's Tomb of Pope Alexander VII; over our heads, the gilded bronze skeleton of Death held aloft an hourglass. Those words from Fitzgerald's *This Side of Paradise* came again to mind: "If it wasn't life, it was magnificent."

At the Frankfurt Book Fair, I got my first taste of international publishing. Virtually every house from all over the world had stands in those halls the size of several football stadiums. We commuted back and forth each day from our hotel in Wiesbaden, where one evening I took off to attend a performance of *Così fan tutte* in an intimate opera house wholly befitting Mozart's confection of musical magic. Then it was on to London to visit an English publisher with more generations than we could boast,

John Murray & Sons, founded in 1768. The current head had a young grandson and namesake nicknamed "Octavo"—the eighth! At twenty-four, I felt very young indeed.

Back in the States later that fall, Scott and Zelda were reburied in a Catholic cemetery in Rockville, Maryland, as I was commuting back and forth to Princeton's library to research my new edition, scheduled for the next spring list, of his only published play, *The Vegetable*. It received some nice reviews and even prompted a few playhouse productions in the years to come. In a more dramatic reprise of Fitzgerald that year, Elia Kazan's splendid, and underrated, film *The Last Tycoon* hit the screens. Robert De Niro played Monroe Stahr to perfection. Overly protective of our copyright, I denied Harold Pinter's request to allow his screenplay to be published; I wanted people to read Fitzgerald instead. I was wrong, but I was young. Years later I relented. It's a superb dramatic adaptation and well worth reading.

In May, my father received the Curtis Benjamin Award for Creative Publishing, largely for his role in producing eminent reference sets. I had been taking a day or so each week of unpaid leave to work in the art library at my old department, where I had recently been hired to teach two days a week that coming fall as a preceptor (instructor) in John Rupert Martin's Baroque course. At its high-water mark a few years later, it would be ranked the most popular course in the university, with an enrollment of three hundred students. My sights were still divided between publishing and the university. But I had no idea what I was going to do for a dissertation, the prerequisite for a post someday as a professor.

I had my own "Eureka!" moment right after reunions in early June, Princeton's bacchanalia for alumni. I would take my Princeton senior thesis and rewrite it over the summer before teaching began. I did not take any days off from Scribners; I just got to the office earlier each morning and wrote for two hours until the mail was delivered and my day job began. By summer's end, the dissertation was finished, all two hundred pages. I shifted to a three-day week at Scribners while teaching, and the dissertation was defended and the degree awarded in December before the end of classes. I have never worked so fast. Giving up drinking was half the secret; the other was my dad's dictum, "No rush, just do it now."

By the end of that bifurcated year of publishing and teaching, I had been put in charge of the Scribner Library paperbacks, which now included not only literary classics but the whole range of our hardcover publishing—from novels to needlecraft and everything in between. That job meant that I got to deal with authors (and estates) that I had had no role in bringing to the firm. At the same time, my father had not given up his love of hardcovers; he lamented the fact that so many classic titles could not be kept in print in hardcover since the demand was lower than the minimum quantity that justified going back to press. So he launched a new line of high-quality "library" hardcovers—like university press books—that could be printed in lower quantities; he called them "Hudson River Editions." I was put in charge of "converting" titles to this series, which required that I write the authors for their approval (they would get full royalties, but at a lower rate, to enable going back to press for smaller print runs— the only way the series could work). One of my first reissues was our biography of the newly canonized Elizabeth Ann Seton, the first American saint.

On a much lighter note, I took on some "art books"—all in glorious black and white, a recapitulation of those "Gibson Girl" books published early in the century by my great-grandfather: four collections of cartoons by *The New Yorker* cartoonists Henry Martin, Dana Fradon, and Nurit Karlin. These had been prefaced by a small book I signed up from England by my favorite equestrian cartoonist, Norman Thelwell, whose books featuring young children on fat ponies I had devoured a decade earlier with my cousins at Woodcott. It was called *Brat Race*. A few months later in 1976, Princeton alumnus Henry Martin, whose one-room studio sat across the street from the gates of the Princeton University Press, submitted to my dad two collections of his *New Yorker* cartoons: one on business, the other on marriage. They were titled, respectively, *Good News/Bad News* and *Yak! Yak! Yak! Blah! Blah! Blah!* The former landed this whimsical artist a syndicated newspaper series with the same title that I had given the book. He was the easiest author I ever dealt with, as delightful as his cartoons.

Upstairs on the eighth floor, my father had signed up and was now translating from the German a small book of devastating satirical essays by Gabriel Laub, all illustrated by the equally incisive graphic artist Hans Georg Rauch, called *Double-Barreled Attack*—in the tradition of Jonathan Swift and H. L. Mencken. He also published Rauch's book of captionless, exquisite etchings, *Battlelines*, a worthy successor to M. C. Escher. I still treasure the artist's proof he inscribed to my father; it shows a tiny Baroque church with a large "thought balloon" of Baroque embellishments that demolishes the modernist glass-and-steel office buildings surrounding it. The year before, Dad had made his own translation from the original German of the Brothers Grimm's *Hansel and Gretel*, illustrated by Adrienne Adams, whose *Woggle of Witches* had been such a success for Scribners' juvenile division. The copyeditor took issue with his translation of *steinalt* as "old as the hills." It was in fact an inspired equivalent, but she marked it "cliché." My father, less than amused, pointed out that the tale was very old and that clichés were once young. It remained, *stet*.

Early in January 1977, when I had corrected my last Princeton exams and returned to the office full time, I was joined by a new recruit from Yale: Stuart Johnson. He was the most brilliant colleague among a group of young assistant editors, and we became fast friends to this day. We worked together on Dana Fradon's collection of cartoons and titled them *Insincerely Yours*—a nod to my father, who often quipped, "The depths of my insincerity have yet to be plumbed." (It's a required diplomatic skill for a publisher.) For Nurit Karlin's collection of captionless *New Yorker* cartoons, we came up with *No Comment.* A year and a half later, Stuart would pursue his true calling, like my brother Blair, as a teacher. Within a decade he would be the youngest and most celebrated headmaster in the city and serve in that post for thirty-five years. But before he moved on, I introduced him to an equally gifted assistant in publicity a floor above us, Susan O' Connell—his future wife. She would leave publishing for a distinguished career in law and banking. Scribners was also a farm team.

The year had begun auspiciously with the publication of the *Scribner-Bantam Dictionary.* We sold the hardcover; they, the paperback. As a footnote to history, it was the first dictionary to list Jimmy Carter as president. In fact, it did so before the election results; the tight printing schedule required finished proofs before November. The editors gave the future president an entry before the voters decided. It was a gamble, but it worked out. I sent President Carter a copy with a note explaining this "first." He sent back a most gracious reply.

That winter I set my sights on a new career. I leapt at the chance to apply for a full-time position at Princeton as an assistant professor, tenure track, to continue to teach Baroque art under Professor Martin. As part of my campaign for the job, I delivered a paper on Caravaggio's *Supper at Emmaus* in February at the College Art Association meeting in Los Angeles, which was followed by its publication in *The Art Bulletin.* Jacques Barzun was my final editor on that article. It is still in print today, forty-five years later, in the anthology *Art, Creativity, and the Sacred*—thanks to Jacques. The next month I flew to Sarasota, Florida, to give my first public lecture—on Rubens's Eucharist tapestries—followed by a gallery talk on the huge preparatory canvases, the glory of the Ringling Museum. It was filmed for a PBS television series on the museum.

I didn't get the post. The senior faculty wanted me, but the junior members voted no. They had come from outside universities to compete on Princeton's tenure track. I was the homegrown lad with inside tracks: a protégé of the department chairman, Jack Martin, and, worse, a friend of the university president, Bill Bowen. My father was a charter trustee. I don't blame them. They had good reasons to want me out. So out I went, back to publishing—by default.

Upon my return, Barzun told me I was better off staying where I was. "Academic politics are especially mean," he said.

"Why?" I asked.

"Because the stakes are so small."

Be careful what you pray for—you may get it. I did not, and I consider that a blessing now. Had I gotten that post at Princeton I would never have returned for good to my beloved zip code in New York. I would not have spent so many evenings over the next two years at the Metropolitan Opera, where I met the legendary assistant manager known as "Mr. Met," Francis Robinson, who became my mentor and guide through that musical paradise. My original intention was to get a memoir from Francis; he demurred: "I'd have to leave New York if I ever wrote that book." I didn't get an opera book, but I gained an invaluable friend at the Met.

On one tour of the opera house, Francis pointed out a striking bronze bust of the legendary Antonio Scotti as Scarpia in *Tosca*. For once, I had something to contribute: "He was my father's godfather." Scotti and Caruso, about whom Francis had written a book, were not only a famous duo on stage but close friends off stage in those early years of the century, the Golden Age of the Met. Scotti was also a favorite guest of my grandparents in Far Hills. Once, my grandmother told me, she was on the phone in the front hall and he started singing full voice upstairs in the shower. She couldn't hear a word on the line and shouted, also in full voice, "Will you be quiet!" Scotti came downstairs dripping wet and roared with laughter: "The Met pays me thousands of dollars to sing every night, and I come out here and you tell me to shut up." He later found it equally puzzling that my grandmother declined his invitation to travel to Italy with him—sans husband and children.

That winter Alan Paton came over from South Africa. I was commissioned to be his driver out to Princeton where he was giving a lecture. En route along the New Jersey Turnpike, Paton kept pestering me to identify the bare trees as we passed them. (I wouldn't have known them even with their leaves.) After the third "I don't know," I replied in exasperation, "OK, *you* tell *me* what they are." Silence from the back seat, then Mrs. Paton said, "Ah, Charlie, finally you've learned how to deal with Alan." He and my father were fond of each other, and Dad admired his idealism and courage in standing up to the South African government. But he could be the most prickly and difficult author. Once, alone, my father asked me, "Why can't God make *good* people *nice?*" When my parents took the Patons out to dinner they wisely enlisted their favorite of my girlfriends—my future wife, Ritchie—to come along as my date to ensure that Alan behaved. She was likewise recruited to entertain Mary Hemingway. I was getting a message.

Later that fall, after returning from the Frankfurt Book Fair with my father—and finally moving into my own apartment all of two blocks away from home—I got an unusual invitation from Francis to be his guest at "Pipe Night" at the Players Club. He had arranged the evening's entertainment by three opera stars; two of them, the tenor and baritone, sat at the table with us. The third, soprano Mary Costa, was singing Musetta at the Met that month; she was his longtime friend and fellow Tennessean, who had been singing that role on the Met tour of Japan with Francis two years earlier. She was upstairs resting in Edwin Booth's bedroom as we all listened to a rare recording (from a wax cylinder) of the famous actor—and brother of Abraham Lincoln's assassin—reciting Shakespeare. Francis was irritated that his star soprano was still upstairs and so he sent me to fetch her. I climbed halfway up and then decided I was not about to invade her privacy. I called out and explained that Francis was concerned about her. She replied that she was just avoiding a room full of smokers and would be down shortly—through the kitchen to the stage. I returned to the table and reported that the soprano would be down on time: "They're just stringing the wire for her to make a dramatic entrance," I added.

Mary sang Violetta's aria and duet "Libiamo" from *Traviata*. We were all swept away. On the cab ride with Francis back to her hotel, she and I (trying to be gallant) struggled over who would hold her suitcase. I asked her if I might be on the list to visit her backstage after one of her *La Bohème* performances; I went to them all, and backstage too. At one of them, I brought along Phyllis (P. D. James), who had come over at my father's invitation to go on a national tour organized by his enthusiastic publicity director Susan Richman for her latest Adam Dalgliesh mystery and first bestseller: *Death of an Expert Witness*. We presented Musetta a copy in her dressing room after the performance. The next night at dinner, the new "Queen of Crime" announced to my parents (I was at the opera) that there was something brewing backstage. I was clueless; Phyllis was the master of clues. She was two months ahead of me.

Mary became my musical muse and was responsible for my reading Marcia Davenport's first Scribner novel, *Of Lena Geyer*. She told me on my first visit to her and her mother in Beverly Hills that she had once been approached by a producer at Paramount to star in a film of it. She declined; the part was for a dark European diva (Callas would have been perfect). Mary was an all-American blonde from Tennessee. But out of curiosity I got the Scribner Library paperback as soon as I was back in New York and read it nonstop. Then during that bicoastal year of 1978 I read all of Marcia's other novels on the plane back and forth to Los Angeles between Mary's opera and concert tours. On one trip, I flew up to Monterrey to have lunch with Marcia, who was then living in Carmel. I reminded her that when we first met at my father's launch party for Hemingway's *Islands in the Stream*, she had told me that if I joined the firm—as the fourth Charles Scribner in her publishing life—she would write me a novel.

Marcia protested that fiction was for the young; at seventy-five, she was too old, she insisted, to write another novel. Her last book, *Too Strong for Fantasy* (1967), was the celebrated memoir I found so riveting. "But," I protested, "I've just finished Graham Greene's latest novel, and he's the same age."

She replied, "There's a big difference: He never stopped writing them."

I didn't get my book, but I did get a superb introduction by Marcia for my reissue of the letters of her beloved Max Perkins: *Editor to Author*.

I was now in charge of subsidiary rights at Scribners—selling licenses to paperback reprinters for our titles—so I took it upon myself to see that all Marcia's books were brought back into print. The novels were reissued by Popular Library (P. D. James's paperback publisher; that gave me some clout), and the two non-fiction titles (*Mozart* and her memoir) by Avon Books, whose publisher, Walter Meade, was already a friend and frequent guest of mine at the Met. He became another mentor, calling himself "Uncle Walter," with abundant avuncular advice. I recall vividly, during an intermission of *Traviata*, Walter advising me: "Never confuse romance with marriage; all great romance ends in tragedy—usually death. Can you imagine Shakespeare's play ending with Romeo and Juliet raising their children in a suburban house outside Verona?" Marcia, in turn, had the last word. Upon hearing that all her books were now back in print, she said, "Charlie, it just goes to show: If an author lives long enough, it's as good as being dead."

My field was—and is—the Baroque. But the most memorable artist-author in my life that year was decidedly modern: Louise Nevelson. In 1976 we had published her book of memoirs in conversation with her assistant and photographer Diana MacKown:

Dawns + Dusks. Now it was time for me to publish the paperback. The year before, her sculptural chapel for St. Peter's Church at the Citicorp complex had been unveiled to rave reviews. I loved it. I consider it to this day the finest chapel this side of the Atlantic, a worthy successor to Matisse's Rosaire Chapel at Vence. Her serene white wooden relief sculptures combine her characteristic abstraction with evocative Christian iconography—by a Jewish artist, for a Lutheran church—intended to appeal to visitors of all faiths; she herself called it a spiritual "oasis." I wanted our paperback to feature a stunning black-and-white photograph of Louise standing within it. Diana MacKown obliged, and it remains one of my favorite covers. At lunch after the photo shoot, I asked Louise, cluelessly, "Are your eyelashes artificial?" (Her signature flourish, they measured more than an inch.) *"Everything* about me is artificial," she replied. Now her turn, she asked, "Tell me, Charles, is this the *real world* we are in?" An impossible question. Either way, I would sound either lacking in spiritual imagination or demented. After a long pause, I said, tentatively, "Well, I'm not sure, Mrs. Nevelson, but I think it's the closest we'll get to it in this lifetime." She approved.

The biggest event for our corporate history that year came in the summer with the announcement of our merger with the publishing house Atheneum, headed by Alfred (Pat) Knopf Jr., son of the famous Knopf publishers, Alfred and Blanche. Atheneum had an impressive history of bestsellers; they also had a superb children's book department. Scribners would be the majority partner—we were considerably larger—but each side would enjoy editorial autonomy. At a time when conglomerates were snapping up publishing houses, this solution seemed promising to maintain our independence and yet have more heft in the competitive marketplace. My father liked and admired Pat, and Lee Rodgers, who orchestrated the merger, was very collegial with his counterpart at Atheneum, Marvin Brown.

We all had high hopes, and the press was good. But it would prove to be less than an ideal marriage. Pat had cofounded Atheneum in 1959 following a break with his father at Knopf; he never would be happy unless he were boss. My father was now chairman—and majority shareholder—of the new corporate entity, "The Scribner Book Companies." Pat was vice-chairman. But he saw himself as the senior publisher, both in years and in wisdom. As a youth he had been so despondent when turned down by Princeton that he ran off to Salt Lake City. I can't help but wonder now how uneasy it might have felt to be at a house so closely tied to Princeton, working alongside a charter trustee. The more troubling consequences of this merger lay several years in the future. But in the end, that friction would produce the best of all outcomes, a much bigger merger less than six years later that would prove as profitable for our family as promising for the future of the Scribner imprint.

In the fall that followed, Scribners published one of the most beautiful and poetic books in its history—a fusion of art, mysticism, and nature: *Of Wolves and Men*, by Barry Lopez. It was a collaboration and labor of love by the inspired author and his editor, Laurie Graham, who would later become my father's cousin by marriage to the widowed George Schieffelin. Lopez, like Eiseley, would go on to be celebrated as "another Thoreau." After the successes of Dubos, Eiseley, and now Lopez, we were firmly rooted in the field of environmental books, works that celebrate nature with the power of poetry. This sumptuous debut on our list would be fully recognized eight years later with Lopez winning a National Book Award for his next Scribner book, *Arctic Dreams*, in 1986. His *New York Times* obituary in 2020 cited these two books as "works of extraordinary immersive rigor, imaginative breadth and intellectual depth." His Jesuit education was not in vain. His early hero, Teilhard de Chardin, would have approved.

My father, in the meantime, had penned his first children's book, a retelling of the old tale *The Devil's Bridge*. Illustrated by

Evelyn Ness, it received good reviews, especially within our family. The most colorful character was the mayor's wife, who invariably agrees with and repeats everything her husband says. Thereafter at home, we referred to my mother as "the mayor's wife." She concurred.

The new year brought the first of several reference sets coming off press after years of preparation: the first two (of eight) volumes of *British Writers*, edited by Ian Scott-Kilvert—the first of many to benefit from the editorial genius of Barzun. A month later, the miniseries *From Here to Eternity* hit TV screens. Starring William Devane and Kim Basinger, it almost put us out of business—or so I had feared a few months before. The problem, no one's fault, lay in the new Copyright Act of 1976, which gave heirs to an author's copyright the right to renegotiate terms, or change publishers, if the author died before its renewal. James Jones's estate qualified. He had died in 1975 and the renewal would not come up until 1979.

Scribners had earlier and in good faith granted a reprint license to Avon Books for the paperback, and Avon had several years left, enough to plan a big tie-in edition with the upcoming miniseries. Meanwhile, Jones's widow, Gloria, had reclaimed all her rights from Scribners and resold them to Dell, which was now simultaneously planning a big paperback reprint timed to the miniseries. Both giant firms felt they had valid claims to proceed with their paperbacks and threatened to sue each other—and Scribners. We were caught in the middle, facing potential legal fees that might put us out of business if this intriguing test case worked its way up to the Supreme Court. That, in any event, was my nightmare as head of subsidiary rights and my father's son. So I called Walter Meade at Avon and begged him to find a solution, some way to call off the Hearst lawyers.

Walter rose to the occasion. He convened a meeting at his office with Lee Rodgers and me along with the Hearst legal eagles. He promised to find an amicable compromise with Dell that would spare us all from litigation. And he was as good as his word: Avon would sell off its remaining stock and relinquish its license; Dell would be the official paperback publisher for the miniseries. I have never been more grateful to a colleague, mentor, and friend. Going to the opera has its rewards. Six years later Walter would be my candidate to become publisher of Scribners under its new corporate parent, Macmillan. Alas, the job would go instead to Pat Knopf's candidate, who would last only two years before becoming an agent, her true calling.

There was a still greater challenge for us as a result of that new law: the fate of the Scott Fitzgerald books. The law granted an extra nineteen years of copyright protection, but authors or their estates would have the option of changing publishers for that extension. We could lose the entire Fitzgerald corpus that my father had so successfully built up from obscurity into bestsellers supporting both our house and the author's daughter, Scottie, and her children. We were prepared to make the most generous offer we could, but it was clear that her top advisers, her agent at Harold Ober and her adviser Matthew Bruccoli, wanted to shop the books around to other publishers for the highest bidder. There would be no lack of interest in such an auction. Bruccoli had for years been complaining that our Scribner editions, especially of *Gatsby*, were corrupt with errors. Fitzgerald indeed had been no speller, and Perkins no copyeditor. But most of the typos had been corrected over the decades by my father. I decided to tackle the charge head on.

Bruccoli had published a handbook explaining all the changes he thought should be made in *Gatsby*. I took it home and proceeded to go through them one by one and mark my copy with all that I thought made sense. I did not agree with every "correction"; for instance, I was not about to change the spelling of Meyer Wolfsheim to "Wolfshiem" just because Fitzgerald had misspelled it in his manuscript (he also spelled Gertrude Stein as "Stien," and a yacht as "yatch"). Nor would I change "retinas" to "irises" or "pupils" in the author's famous description of the billboard eyes of Dr. Eckleburg. Fitzgerald was not an ophthalmologist, and his word choice deserves to be respected. Likewise, Astoria would remain Astoria and not be changed to "Long Island City" at Bruccoli's geographical insistence. Perhaps Fitzgerald preferred the poetic sound of the former or its evocation of the tycoon Astor?

I wrote an introduction to my new 1979 paperback edition and reproduced the original Cugat artwork on the cover, that iconic Art Deco image that graced the first edition and has remained on our paperback for the past forty-four years. I sent the introduction to Scottie, and she approved it. I had to walk a fine line—holding my ground but not in any way criticizing her longtime adviser. Bruccoli, in the meantime, had been hired by publishers Harcourt Brace Jovanovich as their new "consulting editor." Scottie's agent, who was also Bruccoli's agent, admitted to me that they had agreed to let Bruccoli reedit all the books according to his lights for "authorized editions" should they win the bidding to be the new publisher of Fitzgerald's works. I knew what we were up against. I had recently moved into Max Perkins's old office and now had his desk. I also bought a Baldwin upright piano to play there after hours. By springtime, no progress had been made on negotiations with Scottie's agent at Harold Ober and her lawyer.

Several months earlier, Mary Costa had said out of the blue that I would marry my childhood sweetheart, Ritchie Markoe. When I asked why, she replied, "Because you are always speaking of her." By June, Ritchie and I were engaged. The wedding was in August. In between, my father wrote to Scottie directly, around her agent, asking to meet with her to discuss the future of her father's books. He made a persuasive case for staying with the house from which all the schools and colleges were used to ordering their classroom copies—the chief market for Fitzgerald.

Changing publishers after more than fifty years would cause chaos.

That fall, soon after Ritchie and I returned from our wedding trip to England (where P. D. James told my new bride over dinner, "You know, my dear, you have married a very complicated man"), Scottie arrived at my office along with her two daughters, Eleanor and Cecilia, for a meeting with my father and me over a proposed contract. I was guardedly optimistic. Clearly her willingness to come, over the objections of her agent and adviser, spoke to her underlying sense of loyalty and tradition. She came bearing a wedding gift for Ritchie and me, but as soon as she caught sight of my piano she asked me to play her something. So I sat down and played my favorite Chopin waltz (thank God I did not then know its nickname—the "Adieu"). Halfway through it, I had the chilling thought that Fitzgerald's future at Scribners might depend on this waltz. But somehow I made it through without a hitch, and Scottie sighed, "It's all so romantic."

Later upstairs, Scottie told us to proceed with a contract—which remains in effect today for the life of the copyrights. The key requirement of that contract is that Scribners would guarantee minimum annual royalties for the next twenty years. My father had some real concerns about the likelihood—much less certainty—that *Gatsby* would remain required reading in schools and colleges for another generation. He recalled the fate of Eliot's *Silas Marner*, the standard assigned novel of his own schooldays. Would *Gatsby*, now at its high point in sales, hold its place for two more decades? Fortunately, Lee Rodgers came to the rescue and demonstrated that even if sales declined, the math was in Scribners' favor. In fact, as it turned out, throughout the next twenty years the sales would double—an unprecedented apotheosis of an American classic.

The next month, October, we published what would turn out to be Lord Snow's final novel, a murder mystery: *A Coat of Varnish*. I had been appointed the editor of record (he needed no real editing). This newlywed almost upset a great literary marriage—between Snow and Pamela Hansford Johnson—by publishing a literally "unauthorized" dedication in that novel. Our first American edition features the dedication "For Kate Marsh." This innocuous phrase prompted a passionate protest via airmail from the author; he wrote to me that he had never dedicated *any* of his books to *anyone*, not even to his wife. (One can only imagine Lady Snow's reaction to this unique dedication.) Worse, he had no idea who this Kate Marsh was. "Who is she?" he demanded.

I took the red-hot letter to my father. "If his lordship cannot remember whom he dedicates his book to, how can he expect us to know?" was Dad's wry reaction. The manuscript itself yielded no clue, just those dedicatory words clearly penciled on the title page. The mystery was solved by his American agent, James Oliver Brown, a wonderful gentleman of the old school who later became one of my closest friends and mentors in the business.

"Jim, Lord Snow wants to know who Kate Marsh is. Do you have any idea?" I asked.

Jim laughed. "Of course he knows Kate. She's Graham Watson's secretary." The light dawned. When Snow initially sent the manuscript to his London agent, Graham Watson, someone in the mail room had evidently written "For Kate Marsh" to route it to the right office. Later, across the wide Atlantic, those penciled words were given a new interpretation—and their own page—by the Scribner copyeditor, and the rest is bibliographic history. I cannot think of another case where a dedication lasted only one printing. Still, Kate had her moment of acknowledgment.

The new decade began with P. D. James's new novel, *Innocent Blood*, her "breakout book" that transformed both her career and finances. Three years earlier at dinner with my father, Jacek, and me in London, the author explained that she wanted to write something different to follow *Death of an Expert Witness*, a novel that would stand on its own; that is to say, not a who-done-it featuring one of her two detectives, Adam Dalgliesh or

Cordelia Gray (introduced five years earlier in *An Unsuitable Job for a Woman*), but a psychological novel of suspense that would be sold as fiction, not a mystery. She sketched the plot; it was clear her heart was set on it. We gave her our full support, and we were richly rewarded. *Innocent Blood* was an instant bestseller, chosen by the Book-of-the-Month Club as a main selection, and soon became the book that all the paperback houses were clamoring to acquire. Suddenly this new subsidiary rights director—a post I accepted reluctantly when my predecessor left—had his hands full of fun.

Phyllis came over for press interviews, a national tour, and a grand luncheon hosted by the Book-of-the-Month Club. Together with her editor Elinor Parker, the doyenne of our mysteries as well as needlecraft books (I sense a connection but cannot pinpoint it), Phyllis was joined by my father and Scribner executives at the most festive gathering I can recall in thirty years of publishing. She was the star author who sparkled with megawatts. She was also, for the first time in her life, financially independent. For decades she had been working at a succession of government jobs that supported her family after her late husband, a doctor, had come back from the war disabled. Her writing was confined to an hour early each morning before work. Now she could devote herself full time to her craft. My father and I were thrilled. No author ever more deserved these long-deferred financial rewards—and fame.

Our most famous author of all was to have his turn back in the spotlight the next February with the publication of *Ernest Hemingway: Selected Letters: 1917–1961*, edited by Carlos Baker. My father and Baker made the selection for this huge volume together (almost one thousand pages) and collaborated on the editing. It took the public—academics, publishers, Hemingway fans—by surprise. For the twenty years following Hemingway's death, my father and Mary had prohibited the publication—even quotations—of the author's letters. In his memoir, Dad gave the reasons for this reversal, admitting that it would be something "for which I'll have to account to Ernest in the hereafter":

> *Hemingway left strict instructions that his letters should not be published. But with Mary's approval I published them— and I think I did the right thing. To begin with, he had kidded my father about publishing his letters, so he had thought of such a thing. Second, I believe his letters show a side of him that nothing else in his work does, and it is a very nice side. I consider that I was justified. It is well known that Virgil left instructions for his Aeneid to be burned after his death. Fortunately, not all literary executors obey such requests.*

My father and I decided to do something unheard of before publication. I would offer the Book-of-the-Month Club an exclusive look at the manuscript on one condition: If they wanted the book, they had to make it the main selection for the month (most titles were offered as "alternate selections"). Pat Knopf, who relished the wheeling and dealing in subsidiary rights more than the books themselves, was most disapproving, to put it mildly. He told me that I could not do that; the established policy was to offer a book to both the Book-of-the-Month Club and its competitor, Doubleday's Literary Guild. (His recent editor-in-chief of Atheneum was now the Guild's director.) But Dad and I wanted to go for the gold—a main selection or nothing. We got permission from Alfred Rice, Hemingway's lawyer, to proceed, and it paid off. We got our main selection.

Under ordinary circumstances, that would set up an auction for paperback rights (as it recently had for P. D. James). But as I was also in charge of our own paperback line, I preferred to forgo the fleeting glory (and cash) of a big sale and keep the book for our Scribner Library. There would be no auction. Pat was once again beside himself with this son who wouldn't play the game. But I was my father's son, not his. We would be Hemingway's sole publisher, keep the publishing profits, and earn more royalties for Mary. Win, win. It was the heftiest paperback we ever published—and that is still in print.

The most memorable impromptu lunch in my publishing life was with a Hemingway. Attorney Alfred Rice called to tell me that he was sending Hemingway's youngest son, Gregory, to have lunch with my dad and me. Gregory, he explained, had been kicked out of the Plaza Hotel and went to Mary Hemingway's apartment, half a mile away, in the middle of the night. Mary sat up with him all night, terrified, holding a kitchen knife. He was in a manic state. All she had in her fridge was a quart of milk and a quart of vodka. By the time Gregory arrived at my office, he had calmed down but was still dressed in a green velour 1970s jogging suit (since the Plaza would not let him back in his room). Dad was a sport and suggested we walk two blocks south to a Japanese restaurant. Gregory was charming the whole way, slowly jogging in place backward down Fifth as he conversed with us. He explained that he could "jog as fast backwards as forwards" and was planning to run in the Boston Marathon backward.

When we got to our table, to make small talk I told him that my father-in-law had his uncle Gus Pfeiffer's desk at the Warner-Lambert pharmaceutical company, where he was vice-chairman. Gregory then regaled us about his visit with the late chairman, Elmer Bobst, at their cosmetics factory. He and his brother Patrick were shareholders through their mother's family (Pfeiffer). Gregory, who was himself a physician, marveled at Bobst's impressive pseudoscientific explanation of the latest facial cream that "penetrated from the epidermis all the way down to the *subdermis.*" Gregory then loudly announced to my dad and me that he was "bisexual." Everyone around us stopped eating and looked at our table, whereupon Gregory asked me, "Is that the right word?"

"Right word for what?" I replied.

"You know, when a batter can hit as easily left-handed or right-handed."

"I think you mean ambidextrous," I offered.

"Yes," he exclaimed, "that's the word I was looking for! I'm *ambidextrous*." We went back to our tempura without further ado.

On April 26, 1981, another Scribner was born: Charles Scribner IV (actually the sixth, but we'd lost count by then). The day he arrived, the *Daily News* ran in its Sunday morning edition a feature on my father and me, photographed outside 597 Fifth, as a publishing team. Another Charles was now waiting in the wings—of New York Hospital. "Coincidences are God's way of remaining anonymous." Once again, Einstein got it right.

In January 1982 I became publisher of our new paperback division. I was glad to hand over subsidiary rights to a young assistant who had selling and negotiating in her blood. I was born for neither. That month Rawson Associates joined the company as a second new division. Ken and Eleanor Rawson had a gift for publishing commercial bestsellers; their most recent killing was with *The Complete Scarsdale Medical Diet*. Its author, Dr. Herman Tarnower, alas had been murdered in 1980 by his mistress, Jean Harris. A decade later, Scribners would publish Harris's own book, written in prison. So we ended up publishing both sides, victim and killer—a publishing first, if not award worthy.

That year would see a new plaque on our building. The New York City Landmarks Preservation Committee designated it, over our objections, a city landmark. It was to prove more a curse than an honor. We never doubted that the Flagg building was a treasured landmark; we had preserved it as such for seventy years. But the official designation came with yards of red tape that would soon prove burdensome in maintaining the building as a functioning publishing house and store, not a museum. Yet within a couple of years that burden would also prompt a positive move forward.

Inside 597 Fifth, newer monuments were appearing, the ones "more durable than bronze," as a series of reference books: *Science Fiction Writers*, *Ancient Writers: Greece and Rome*, the first volume of the *Dictionary of the Middle Ages*, followed the next year by the first two (of fourteen) volumes of *European Writers*. My father's vision of his sequential reference works as "modular," that is, expanding and complementing each other, was taking form.

If one year, and only one, could be seen as pivotal to the history of Scribners since its founding as a family firm in 1846, my choice would be 1983, which began with two key departures. First, our treasurer, Marvin Brown, left to become head of New American Library paperbacks. Then, our president, Lee Rodgers, followed suit to become president of Warner Publishing Services, an opportunity too good to pass up. My father and I were at first, and understandably, shaken by these departures. But at his farewell party, Lee made a characteristically positive remark that would prove prophetic: "Changes bring opportunities." My father, the chairman, resumed his post as company president and CEO; he appointed Jacek president of the Charles Scribner's Sons division (Pat remained head of Atheneum), and I became executive vice president and secretary. I moved, along with my piano, from Max's office to the eighth-floor executive suite.

As corporate secretary, I was in charge of all matters concerning the board and administration, including legal. I was also in charge of the bookstore, which was owned by our family but separate from the publishing house. Finally, I was responsible for the house itself, the recent landmark. My father and Jacek, who had worked hand in glove for so many years, presided over our publishing programs. Remembering Lee's remark, I took heart. It was all new to me. I had no background in finance. My doctorate in art history was no substitute for an MBA. But I had a plan that I had been mulling over for the past three years.

I was very close to Ritchie's father, Frank Markoe, whom I had known many years before he became my father-in-law.

He was a brilliant lawyer who had become general counsel and vice-chairman of the pharmaceutical company Warner-Lambert. He had come from Baltimore to New Jersey with his two young daughters in the mid-1950s after merging their mother's family business, the Emerson drug company, into Warner-Lambert. Emerson, maker of Bromo-Seltzer, had a proud tower in Baltimore (which stands to this day) but was suffering from competition with the large, publicly owned drug companies. Mr. Markoe (as I always called him since childhood) transformed the family fortunes by making that merger for stock, not cash, over the objections of several relatives. When Warner-Lambert was eventually acquired by Pfizer, his brilliance and foresight were confirmed. I saw enough parallels with our situation as a family publishing company to seek a similar outcome. My father's favorite maxim, from the Stoic philosopher Seneca, was "Fate leads the willing and drags the unwilling." I preferred now to be led by reason, not later dragged by necessity. The days of private family publishing firms were clearly numbered, as history would confirm.

My task of persuading my father to think the unthinkable was made far easier by the in-house friction with Pat Knopf. It was clear that we were no longer truly a "family" company. I told my father that I had no desire to stay on after him and preside over such a confederation. I had come on board as his son, not a servant to outsiders. For his part, his sense of duty to his family far outweighed any wish to remain in charge for a few years longer. His ego was grounded in "the life of the mind," not a CEO title. In July, we hired a brilliant financial executive to serve as our new treasurer: Allan Rabinowitz. He had earlier served as the chief financial officer for the Macmillan Publishing Company. As soon as he settled into his new office, he persuaded us to go see the Macmillan warehouse and shipping and billing operation in southern New Jersey. (We had recently sold our facility in Totowa and now remained there as a customer of the new owners.) Allan believed we could save a lot by moving our operations to Macmillan as *their* customer.

Meanwhile, I was quietly pursuing selling our building on Fifth. I saw no advantages to running it with golden handcuffs as a landmark. The bookstore was a jewel, but a pricey one; our family had been subsidizing it for years by charging rent much lower than market value for that prime retail space. (It would be cheaper to own a yacht or a private plane.) Just at this moment during lunch break I happened to spot an artist across Fifth Avenue, sitting at his easel, at work on a painting. I went up to him and recognized the superb "master of cityscapes" Kamil Kubik. My wife, Ritchie, had introduced me to this delightful Czech artist several years earlier. He was now doing a pastel of our Scribner building—for his own pleasure. I said at once that I had to buy it, and I did. I used it on the sales brochure for the building, took it home, and have enjoyed it for the past forty years. It is now on the cover of this book and remains, more than any photo or memory, my "constant image" of 597 Fifth. As Oscar Wilde said, "Life imitates art." The art endures.

Allan then found us a magnificent space to rent on lower Fifth Avenue, just a block south of our original Flagg building. Several other publishers were moving southward; we were just going with the flow. But what to do with the store? I couldn't bear to see its loyal employees lose their jobs. I went looking for a new location. I scoured several sites—from the Singer Sewing store overlooking my mother's ice rink at Rockefeller Center to the belowground level—euphemistically called the "concourse"—of the new Trump Tower.

I made an appointment to tour the bare space with Donald Trump, who was as charming as unconvincing. When I worried aloud about the amount of foot traffic on that basement level (eventually a Tower Records store that went bankrupt), he replied, "I get more traffic through this building every day than the rest of Fifth Avenue from here to Saks." A great line, but not to a

New Yorker who walked and worked on Fifth every day. Three years later at the opening of Trump Rink in Central Park, I met him again—this time with my parents. My mother was performing at the grand opening of the restored Wollman Rink, which Trump had finished in record time after years of delay by the city. I pointed her out to him as she was warming up: "That's my mother; she's a professional figure skater and will be performing for you tonight. She just told me that she thinks *you* should be the mayor of New York." His reply was as good as true: "Charles, your mother would say that about anyone who finished this rink."

Meanwhile our tour of the Macmillan shipping center was most encouraging and Allan proceeded to draw up a contract. As soon as it was signed, I asked my father, "Since we're moving out of our building and shipping our books through Macmillan, why don't we consider merging our company into theirs? We could ensure the future of our imprint and programs without these crushing interest rates from bank loans." (They were then in the double digits.) We were undercapitalized and yet not about to contribute fresh family funds to a company that was no longer "all family." More to the point, I added, "I'd much rather work for a corporation I admired and had shares in than continue working for the bank and minority shareholders who don't share our vision."

My father followed up at once and scheduled a meeting with Macmillan Publishing's president, Jeremiah Kaplan, whom he had known and admired for years; they shared a love of reference books. Jerry was thrilled at the prospect of a merger that would add the Scribner imprint to Macmillan. My father was insistent that we were not selling for cash; he wanted stock in Macmillan. His reason? "I wanted to keep the firm in the book business," he later explained, "and I wanted to maintain my commitment— financially as well as professionally—to a *publishing* company." If the reasons were idealistic, they would yield a windfall: Four years later, the Macmillan stock would be worth *six times* as much. "It must have been my guardian angel who inspired the arrangement," he concluded.

Allan Rabinowitz would be negotiating with Jerry Kaplan, his former boss at Macmillan. He knew their finances as well as ours, so the negotiations never got stuck in misconceptions. Allan was phenomenal, much tougher than either my father or I could ever bring ourselves to be. To strengthen his hand, I suggested to my father that he promote Allan from treasurer to president (and grant him generous stock options for further incentive) to be on an equal level with Kaplan across the table. When the financial matters had been settled, I joined the final meetings representing my father on all the remaining corporate and publishing details of the merger. I loved those meetings. Sitting beside me was a very bright and equally nice (but firm) attorney from Weil, Gotshal & Manges, Susan Poland; we became instant friends. Opposite was Macmillan's general counsel, Beverly Chell, whom I soon viewed not as an adversary but as my future colleague. My main concern was to ensure that the merger was as smooth and positive as possible. I already felt like a member of a new and larger family. If all this sounds like poor negotiating techniques, I'd just stress that I had Allan and Susan as the "bad cops" with all the ammunition they needed to make their cases. Someone had to play "good cop." I was glad to oblige. I wanted only one thing: to get the deal done.

The press coverage of the announced merger was most favorable. I described it to *Time* magazine as a "marriage." It would soon prove a happy one. Macmillan books were originally introduced and distributed in America by Charles Scribner in 1859. A hundred and twenty-five years later we had come full circle.

CHAPTER 13

Mergers and Acquisitions

AFTER THE CONCLUSION OF THE MACMILLAN MERGER IN JUNE, I was called downtown to federal court and selected as a juror for the trial of two mafiosi in a cocaine smuggling deal that went down at a West Side diner. The two defendants, Cleveland crime boss Allie Calabrese and San Francisco underboss Frank ("Skinny") Velotta, were found guilty. That weeklong trial was more than adequate preparation for my transition from the family cocoon on Fifth to my new office on Third as Jeremiah Kaplan's new apprentice. I was there to be groomed in all matters Macmillan. It was like dialing the clock back nine years, but without my dad. I was soon given a new Macmillan title, "Vice President, Special Projects." But I was really there to be weaned from Scribners and trained in corporate practices at the parent firm. Jerry was a good boss, a brilliant publisher, but often inscrutable. Unlike my dad or Jacek, he reveled in being unpredictable, he thrived on ambiguity. I never quite knew where I stood or what he wanted of me. But it was heady, and new, and I was eager to learn.

Jerry erected a barrier between his publishing division and the corporate parent, Macmillan, Inc., on "the tenth floor." But I felt equally at home upstairs since I had a good friend, Jamie MacGuire, in corporate development and had met the corporate chiefs—Chairman Ned Evans and President Bill Reilly and

General Counsel Beverly Chell—in recent months of negotiation. Those ties would prove vital a couple of years later when Jerry would depart for good, unceremoniously.

One thing was clear: Jerry had no plan to send me back to Scribners, which would soon be moving downtown. My furniture would go south to the new offices, but I would not be sitting in my empty office on Fifth. In the meantime, outside my new Macmillan office that summer, I was concluding the sale of our Scribner Building in August and trying to find a savior for the bookstore. I wanted to save the employees' jobs—a mission surely fueled by that summer of '71 working with them. Ritchie was responsible for the next "Eureka!" moment that solved the problem.

Ritchie gave me a beautiful art book on Rome for our August wedding anniversary. Yet the bookstore wrapping paper was not ours, but Rizzoli's, a few blocks north on Fifth. She told me that she had shared with their manager the problem of finding a new home, or owner, for our store. That proved a better present than the book. The next day I called Rizzoli's president, Gianfranco Monacelli, and visited him in his office. I proposed that Rizzoli take over our store. He was, by coincidence, already planning to move his store and offices to a new site on West Fifty-Seventh, the old Sohmer Piano Building. But he was interested in having a larger presence on Fifth by buying our store, leasing the space from the new owners, and also leasing offices in our soon-to-be-vacant building. The price was right. I was willing to sell him the store— inventory, fixtures, and trademark—for a pittance since I really had nothing but the trademarked bookstore name to sell; without a new lease, the rest was worthless to us—but not to Rizzoli. It was done in a handshake, and I was able to persuade Macmillan's chairman, Ned Evans, to approve it as good PR for his new publishing imprint.

A few months later, I would again approach Rizzoli to produce under the Rizzoli music label the only record I've ever coproduced: Betty Buckley's first album, recorded at St. Bartholomew's

Church that June when the Macmillan merger was finalized. My parents had invited Ritchie and me to go with them to hear Betty, the recent Tony Award winner, as Grizabella singing "Memory" in *Cats*. Betty became a friend, and later reissued a fifteenth-anniversary CD of the album. It pays to accept invitations from one's parents.

Before my father and Scribners moved that fall from 597 Fifth, I had two memorable occasions to revisit my old home. The first was to bring novelist James Michener to meet my father that fall. Dad had been working with his young editor Michael Pietsch on preparing Hemingway's *The Dangerous Summer* for publication. Michael, today CEO of Hachette USA and a legendary editor-publisher, edited the text as brilliantly as his predecessors had *Islands in the Stream*. But as a nonfiction title about a difficult subject, bullfighting, it needed an engaging introduction. On vacation with Ritchie at Round Hill, Jamaica, earlier that winter, I had read Michener's *Chesapeake* (Ritchie is from Maryland). I read elsewhere that its author was interested in bullfighting and a fan of Hemingway's. (In fact, Michener told me on our way to the office that he had been responsible for the *Life* magazine serialization in 1952 of *The Old Man and the Sea*.) After discussing the proposal with my father, he wrote the most splendid introduction ever for a Hemingway book; the reviewers cited it with special praise.

The second and last revisit to 597 was celebratory, perhaps the most star-studded event ever held in the building. Merchant-Ivory was releasing their latest film, Henry James's *The Bostonians*. I offered to host a small press party on our editorial floor for the film based on a Scribner novel. Ritchie and her great friend—bridesmaid and godmother to our son Charlie—Jannie Gerrish also came, accompanied by husbands. But the wives would have been happy to go alone to see the film's star, Christopher Reeve, better known as Superman. (He and Jannie had dated as teenagers in Princeton.) It was a fanfare of adieu to our landmark—and in a major key.

The Dangerous Summer was published in June of 1985, a dangerous one for Scribners. That spring, a new publisher was in place—not my candidate, Walter Meade, but Pat Knopf's: Mildred Marmur, the doyenne of subsidiary rights at Random House. Pat had convinced Jerry Kaplan, my new boss, to put him in charge of all trade publishing at Scribners as well as Atheneum. My father would be retiring the next year, and his focus was—and would remain—on reference publishing. For Pat, publishing books was chiefly a prerequisite for making subsidiary rights deals, his forte. His choice for a new publisher at Scribners, a surprise to others in the industry, fit the bill. But the price would prove high. Pat soon drove out our most talented young editor, Michael Pietsch, before his Hemingway triumph was published. William Kennedy, channeling the famous author in his positive *New York Times* review, wrote: "Here we have a great writer who set out to write an epilogue that turned into a book-length manuscript that died of unwieldiness but was later edited to its literary essence and became a book, truly, and is here with us now, and is good."

Before he left, Michael had read the next Hemingway manuscript, *The Garden of Eden*, and persuaded my dad that it deserved to be edited and published, as indeed it would be a year later—but alas not by him. Instead a new editor was hired from *Esquire Magazine*. His drastic reduction of the manuscript by two-thirds made for a brisk, readable novel—but not without complaints from critics. (He cut out two of the main characters, and most of the complexity, in the fine tradition of magazine excerpts.) One can only imagine how Michael would have tackled it. If my father had nothing to do with that editing, he had his hand in another *Garden* that year—*The Garden of the Sphinx* by Pierre Berloquin, a book of "150 Challenging and Instructive Puzzles," which Dad translated from the original French. The former classics scholar and cryptanalyst was not to be limited to Latin, Greek, and German.

The second loss was more noted—and lamented—at the time. In the negotiations to publish P. D. James's next novel, *A Taste for Death*, the new Scribner publisher insulted our most beloved author by lecturing her "as a magistrate" (which Phyllis had become in England) about her legal obligations under the option clause in the contract for her last mystery, *The Skull Beneath the Skin*. At the time of the Macmillan merger, Phyllis wrote a warm and congratulatory letter to my father, expressing all her years of gratitude and affection, but noting that she did not consider herself "chattel" that would automatically pass to Macmillan. Alas, that is how she felt treated by the new regime. Her later books would all be published by Knopf; the future Baroness James would remain a close family friend and visit us on all her trips to New York for her new publishers, and we would reciprocate each time we went to London. The professional had become personal.

But uptown at Macmillan, my life brightened that summer with the arrival of the new religion editor I had recruited from Random House's Ballantine division: Michelle Rapkin. Jerry had put me in charge of reviving Macmillan's (and Scribner's) program of religious book publishing. I set out to find the perfect editor, and I found her at Epiphany Books—of all poetic places. When we first met during this search, she presented me with my favorite short book from childhood, *The Story of the Other Wise Man*, by Scribner author Henry Van Dyke. Epiphany indeed.

Our first project was a book I had long wanted to commission: an anthology of the best of Paul Tillich, the Lutheran theologian (and Scribner author) I had studied in depth my last semester at St. Paul's. The book idea may have been triggered by the more recent publication (not by us) of an anthology—*Art, Creativity, and the Sacred*—which included my 1977 article on Caravaggio's *Supper at Emmaus* together with Tillich's classic piece "Art and Ultimate Reality," which I had never read until we were paired in a book. A Macmillan colleague, Terry Mulry, suggested to me the perfect editor for the volume: Dr. Forrester Church, son of late senator Frank Church and a renowned preacher and author uptown at All Souls Unitarian. At our first lunch meeting at Macmillan, Forrest left me with a quotation from Tillich that has resonated to this day: "Eternity is not length of time, but *depth* of time." Michelle and I had him over for a follow-up lunch and signed him up to edit *The Essential Tillich*. One reviewer (in *Booklist*) wrote: "With this volume, Paul Tillich joins the ranks of the great Christian theologians such as Augustine of Hippo and Thomas Aquinas." A heady debut for our new department. Alas, a year later Michelle would be recruited back to Bantam, but not before leaving us with a huge future bestseller: *Joshua* by Joseph Girzone. Along with its sequels in the field of Christian fiction, it would sell three million copies. Some parting gift.

That summer of '86, in June, Scottie Fitzgerald died in Montgomery, Alabama, the hometown of her mother, Zelda. I spoke on the phone with her a few days before and felt an era was coming to a close. She called her role as a professional daughter "the best paid part-time job in the world." Now I felt moved to reach out to her long-time adviser and aide-de-camp Matt Bruccoli and send him my condolences. Yes, he had tried to lure her away from Scribners several years back, but I never doubted his devotion to her. So I wrote to him, then called him, and soon we were planning book projects together. The first was a new collection of Fitzgerald short stories, dedicated in memory of Scottie, which one reviewer called "more than enough to re-establish Fitzgerald as a master of the American short story." It remains today the standard collection. We soon followed it with collections of Ring Lardner's baseball stories, the complete writings of Zelda Fitzgerald (introduced by novelist Mary Gordon), and *A Life in Letters: F. Scott Fitzgerald*, hailed by reviewers as "essential reading for a full understanding of Fitzgerald as an artist and a man" and "an accessible self-portrait of the writer." It holds a special place on my shelf of commissioned books: Matt dedicated it to me.

In July of 1986, on his sixty-fifth birthday, my father officially retired from Scribners. Jerry gave him a memorable men's dinner at the Century Association with special colleagues over the years at one long table that covered four decades "in the company of writers." He would remain an unpaid adviser overseeing his beloved reference department; the next year his final Hemingway project, *The Complete Short Stories of Ernest Hemingway*, the Finca Vigía Edition, would appear with his final "Publisher's Preface," a fitting envoi. I felt torn. Should I stay on or move on? At a recent tea together, Phyllis James in no uncertain terms urged the latter. She felt I had served my time and should now pursue my real interests. I had, after all, become a publisher and editor by accident of birth, and those family ties had now loosened. I would remain ambivalent for several years to come, but in the meantime I decided to pursue art history on a parallel track, outside my day job. I was born a Gemini; no harm giving it a try.

Earlier that winter, Ritchie and I had gone with a group of trustees and donors of our New York City public television channel THIRTEEN to Vienna. They would be filming a television special, an opera gala at the *Staatsoper*. I was invited to give an ambulatory gallery talk on Rubens at the Kunsthistorisches Museum: "Going for Baroque." The host of the telecast, opera diva Beverly Sills, stopped me in the lobby of the Sacher Hotel and said how sorry she was to have missed it: "Rubens is my favorite artist!"

"May I ask why?" I said.

"He's the one artist who makes me feel *thin*."

Back in the States, I noticed that the distinguished Abrams series "Masters of Art" still lacked a volume on Rubens. I proposed that I write it. At the time I was lecturing on Rubens at the Met Museum and my Rubens dissertation had been published in 1982 by a university press. I got a contract, and now I too was going for Baroque—but keeping my day job. I'm sure that our family friend and favorite author Louis Auchincloss influenced my decision. My dad had pointed out to me, years before, that Louis wrote his dozens of novels while working at a law firm—even on the subway back and forth to his day job. I would try to follow that pattern, sans subway. I walked to work.

In a few months my routine would be rocked by the sudden departure of my boss, Jerry Kaplan. Without any notice, he told me early one January morning in 1987 that it would be his last at Macmillan. (I later learned that he had had a falling out with chairman Ned Evans and that his contract would not be renewed.) We were all stunned. A few weeks before he had asked me to give him a private tour of the old masters at the Met Museum, at the end of which he bought a silver dreidel to give my five-year-old son. The pieces fell into place. He then counseled me to be sure, the next day, that when I was called to the corporate human resources office upstairs I insist on a generous severance package. I went home and prepared a curriculum vitae outlining what I had done—and would do—for Scribners and Macmillan. It was all unnecessary. The point of the meeting, it soon became clear, was to encourage me to stay on and work for the chairman and president directly. I now had two new bosses. I liked them both—so did my dad—and I intended to stay put. The year would conclude on a still higher note: the birth of our second son, Christopher.

Evans and Reilly gave me some novel assignments as a Macmillan diplomat at large. I was to represent the company at the upcoming annual publishers association meeting in Miami, a role that Jerry Kaplan would have played. Whom did I find sitting next to me on the plane? Jerry. On the editorial front, I started to dream up some new books to commission. There were lots of "acquiring editors" in place; they didn't need another one to have lunch with agents. I didn't count myself a candidate. Up until then, the most important book I ever "acquired" was not for Scribners, but for Princeton University Press: my mentor Julius

Held's magnum opus, *The Oil Sketches of Peter Paul Rubens*. He had been sending me pages of his manuscript over the years ever since we met while I was a graduate student—less for editing, more for my art history critiques. When he was finished and needed a publisher, I steered him to Herb Bailey at Princeton University Press since it was out of the question that Scribners could undertake such a massive two-volume scholarly work with a limited academic market. The costs would be prohibitive; only a not-for-profit publisher could do it. Author and Princeton publisher were equally pleased by the outcome. That award-winning book remains, forty years later, the standard reference work on the subject. I call it the "Rubens Bible."

So now I decided, instead—following my father's example— to pursue some authors on my own, directly. I wrote to Graham Greene, a favorite novelist and fellow Catholic, and asked him whether he might write a book about his faith, his beliefs, and his adoptive church. He wrote back a lovely letter declining, explaining that he would "rather have people dig out my ideas in my fiction." But when I approached Father Andrew Greeley, priest and sociologist and longtime friend going back to my college days, he accepted my proposal to write a book called *The Catholic Myth: The Behavior and Beliefs of American Catholics*. It was well received and I accompanied him to the *Today Show*, a first for me—not for him.

I also invited Robert F. Kennedy Jr. to lunch at Macmillan to persuade him to write a book about saving the Hudson River through Riverkeeper, a New York organization that spawned the world's fastest growing water protection movement, Waterkeeper Alliance. It would prove worth the wait. We published it a decade later, coauthored by John Cronin, the Hudson Riverkeeper. A few years later, our college son and family conservationist Charlie would read the book, work for Bobby as a summer intern (thanks to a referral from his mother), write his Princeton thesis on Waterkeeper history, and move to Birmingham, Alabama, to become director of Black Warrior Riverkeeper. Books shape lives.

Another book I had commissioned several years before, August Heckscher's biography of Woodrow Wilson, the first to make use of all the papers being edited by Arthur Link in the Wilson Presidential Library at Princeton, was still far from complete. My dad sent me a note from the Scribner offices downtown: "I don't know which is less likely—that the author will live to finish it, or I will live to read it." Fortunately both did. When it was finally published in 1991, I received a wonderful letter from former President Nixon, a huge Wilson fan who (according to Professor Link) had read not only all of Wilson's books and articles but also his speeches.

Nixon wrote:

As one who has read most of the biographies of Woodrow Wilson, I would rate August Heckscher's at the top of the list. He is obviously an admirer of Wilson, but lets the reader see his faults as well as his virtues. My impression after reading the book from cover to cover was that Wilson was a leader who won great victories and suffered great defeats. But the key word is "great"—Wilson was a great President and the Heckscher biography does justice to his greatness by letting us see the whole man. In fact, an appropriate subtitle to the book might be "The Real Wilson."

He added a postscript: "Please give my warm regards to Mary Costa. Hers was one of the most memorable performances during our White House years."

I had, by coincidence, recently initiated a lawsuit by Mary against the Disney Company when I learned that she had received no royalties on their best-selling videocassette of *Sleeping Beauty*, her first singing role before becoming an opera star. My years in publishing had taught me to look carefully at royalties, both paid and received. Disney was taking the absurd position that her contractual right to receive royalties on all "recordings and transcriptions" did not apply to videocassettes, which of course included the complete audio track of her recorded voice as Sleeping Beauty—all the songs and dialogue. She had a strong case, but three days before the trial in Palm Beach I called her lawyer and said I wanted it settled. I knew that even if she won, which I thought likely, Disney would bleed her over the coming years with expensive appeals, as indeed they did Peggy Lee after she won a similar suit over the video of *Lady and the Tramp*. Unlike Peggy Lee, Mary had said nothing negative about Disney in the press. They had good reason to settle generously, and they did.

A few years earlier when the *Sleeping Beauty* videotape was first released and our older son, age five, had seen it many times, Ritchie and I brought him to meet Sleeping Beauty herself while we were on vacation in Florida. Upon leaving, he turned to Mary to say goodbye. "Goodbye, Mary, Princess Aurora, Briar Rose, Sleeping Beauty," and then with the spindle and curse in mind added, "Watch out for the pricks." We doubled over in laughter as Mary responded, "Charlie, that's the best advice I've been given since moving here to Palm Beach."

My favorite attorney-author, Louis Auchincloss, prompted my favorite commission of all time: his 1989 book on the Vanderbilts. Louis often loved to tease me as being a "*nonkosher* Vanderbilt" since my mother was a descendent of one of the commodore's daughters, whereas Louis's wife, Adele, was descended from the favorite son, William Henry. From his jest I derived the book *The Vanderbilt Era: Profiles of a Gilded Age*. When the manuscript came in, it was dedicated—in the author's own hand—to me as "worthy descendent of the Commodore and only begetter of these insuing sketches." I was dumbstruck by this borrowing from Shakespeare's famous dedication of his Sonnets—as much as Kate Marsh must have been by her unexpected honor from Lord Snow. The launch party at Macmillan was the most celebrity studded I've ever attended, all thanks to Louis: Jackie Onassis, Arthur Miller, Arthur Schlesinger, Malcolm Forbes—the rest is a blur. By then we had a new owner, the official if absent host: the notorious Robert Maxwell.

Over the summer and into the fall of 1988, Macmillan was the prize in a pitched battle between corporate raider Robert Maxwell, a British publishing pirate crossing the Atlantic to make his mark in New York, and a group of Macmillan's senior officers—Evans, Reilly, and Chell—with the backing of Henry Kravis. The company had been put "into play" for a hostile takeover by the Bass Brothers earlier in the spring. A bidding war ensued, and when the smoke cleared and Maxwell won, the buyout stock price was six times its value from when we came on board four years earlier. It was the end of a fine company, and my father and I were sad at this outcome we never envisioned. But the stockholders didn't complain. And we were still in the publishing business, if now under new ownership.

Maxwell and Evans presided over a gathering of Macmillan executives—on Armistice Day. Maxwell and his sons wore red poppies in their lapels as they introduced themselves. Ned Evans was gracious if muted in his introduction of his successors. Maxwell, in a heavy-handed jest for favor, commented that his interest was solely in *publishing*; turning to Ned (who had a distinguished racing stable) he quipped, "I don't own any racehorses."

Ned mumbled, "*Buy* some."

I chuckled, sotto voce, and thought, "Welcome to the Maxwell empire." The *New York Times* later ran a major story in early 1991 when Maxwell bought the *New York Daily News* and asked me for a comment on the Macmillan takeover. I recalled from my recent book on Rubens the color plate and essay on his "Rape of the Daughters of Leucippus" by the demigods Castor and Pollux. I likened the Maxwell takeover to "a divine abduction as painted by Rubens. Like so many of those it ended quite happily. There was hardly a ripple, much less wave." That phrase would come back to haunt me later that year when the bankrupt Maxwell's body, as big as his appetites, was found in the Atlantic after he fell to his death from his yacht, *Lady Ghislaine*. It must have been quite a splash.

The next day an officious member of Maxwell's public relations department called and scolded me: I was never to make a comment to the press without their permission. I told him to reread my comment; it was more positive than anything else in print about Maxwell. My father and I had been speaking to the *Times* for years, I said, and we had never had a bad experience with them. I would continue to speak with anyone from the *Times*. I never got another call from Maxwell's henchmen. Maxwell had his own solution to controlling his press: He bought his own paper, the *Daily News*. When I later met Himself in the executive dining room, he was effusive and charming. His son Kevin, as deputy director, took over Ned Evans's office, and I soon got to know him, my new boss (once-removed). Oxford educated, he was as quiet and serious as his father was brash. I would have no problems with Kevin.

With the bookstore threatening to close in January because Rizzoli was unable to negotiate a workable new lease for the space, Bill Reilly and I, at Maxwell's behest, went downtown to see whether Barnes & Noble might take over and preserve it. But it wasn't to be. The last image of our historic bookstore appeared a year later in director Whit Stillman's debut film, *Metropolitan*: Behind our display window, a pile of books by Jane Austin catches the attention of the leading actress. That, for me, remains "the constant image" of our beloved store.

In a few years there would be no bookstores on Fifth Avenue in midtown; the rents were too high. But Barnes & Noble did acquire the Scribner Bookstore Company, with Maxwell Macmillan's approval, in January and proceeded to open high-end branch bookstores around the country in shopping malls. The store at 597 would become for a few years Brentano's bookstore, then Benetton clothing, then Sephora cosmetics, and now Club Monaco fashions (owned by Ralph Lauren). What next?

The following spring was much brighter, not only because of the appearance—and celebration—of Louis Auchincloss's Vanderbilt book, but for me personally, on a parallel track, with Abrams's publication of my *Rubens*. The *New York Times* gave it a good review and listed it among the best art books of the year. I had of course the best editor of all for its final polishing—Jacques Barzun. At his hundredth birthday, in 2007, I wrote that thirty years later I would not change a word of that book, not as a boast, but as proof of his lasting gift to a budding author.

June was brighter still. My father had urged Maxwell Macmillan's new divisional head to appoint his protégée Karen Day publisher of Charles Scribner's Sons Reference Books—the first woman ever to head that division, his "crown jewel." Several new series would soon follow, beginning with the groundbreaking *Latin American Writers* (three volumes), *African American Writers*, and *Modern American Women Writers*. Karen would flourish in that post for over a decade. Dad could not have been more thrilled; his legacy was secure.

At this time, my father was preparing his own memoir, *In the Company of Writers: A Life in Publishing*, based on an oral history I had commissioned from Columbia University's oral history program. His interviewer, Joel Gardner, and I converted the transcripts into a manuscript. The problem was that by this time my father was suffering from a neurological condition called Holmes Syndrome, which prevented him from reading and writing. (He consulted the famous neurologist Oliver Sacks, author of *The Man Who Mistook His Wife for a Hat*, who encouraged him, his higher intellectual functions undimmed, to forge ahead. Sacks would later include, with my permission, that session in his book *The Mind's Eye*.) So for reading, he turned to recorded books; for writing, to a personal assistant who would take dictation. Dad spoke better than most authors write. Churchill had dictated his books; there was no reason to lose heart. Scribners' new publisher and editor-in-chief, Robert Stewart, signed up the book. (His greatest contribution to our history would be the novelist Annie Proulx, whom he launched that year with *Heart Songs*.) Dad's book would be published in January 1991 to good reviews; an excerpt was published in the *New York Times Book Review*. Dad too had the best editor of all still in house: Jacques Barzun. The result was a conversational tone (because of course the story had been *told*, not written) polished into print by the Bernini of sculptors in prose.

My main interaction with Robert Maxwell himself, during those three years with a pirate at the helm, was as a result of him wanting a complete *leather-bound* set of all of Hemingway's books to display on his yacht, *Lady Ghislaine*, docked in the East River for entertaining his "friends." I recalled Fitzgerald's description of Gatsby's library with all its uncut (and unread) volumes on display. Fortunately I had earlier licensed the rights to produce such a leather-bound library of Hemingway's works (along with those of Fitzgerald) to Easton Press; they were happy to send me a full set for Maxwell's yacht. He never asked for a set of Fitzgerald.

On the art front, that spring of 1991 would mark a double high point for me. First, the publication by Abrams of my second book for their Masters of Art series: *Bernini*, the first title in that series of painters devoted to a sculptor-architect. But Bernini also painted (a little), and I persuaded Abrams to make an exception for this genius who combined all the arts into "*un bel composto*" (a beautiful blend) or *Gesamtkunstwerk* (total artwork). That book, too, benefited from the fine sculpting of Professor Barzun, who left no page unimproved. *Bernini*, which I reissued in a revised paperback edition in 2014, claims a special place in my cherished family memories. Right after its publication, Romo Books in Far Hills, New Jersey, my parents' local bookshop, arranged a signing party for me together with my father for his recent memoir, *In the Company of Writers*. Father and son sat at the same table, signing their respective books for friends and neighbors; my mother presided over us both.

But Rubens was not to be forgotten. In May 1991, I received a call out of the blue from US Customs Special Agent Dave D'Amato. He wanted me to fly down to Miami to take part in an armed undercover operation to trap art thieves who were fencing a Rubens oil sketch stolen from a Spanish museum. (My eighty-five-year-old mentor Julius Held had "volunteered" me in his place.) So off I flew to Miami and played the role of "art adviser" to a would-be purchaser. I was accompanied to a seedy South Beach hotel—the Ocean Grande, with an "e," the site of the sting and takedown of the four criminals—by Special Agent Hank Blair. His words to me going in would later be a *Newsweek* quote of the week: "Since you're going to die anyway, you won't mind if we use you as a shield?" I shot back, "I'm not sure I want to turn forty anyway" (my birthday was two weeks away). In we went. I was given strict instructions: "Don't talk, just look at the picture, nod, shake your head, whatever. We'll get you out of there, and then we're going to blaze in with our armed agents, but we'll get you out first. Don't say a word. Don't talk to these people."

Agent Blair was wearing a concealed wire and a bulletproof vest; I had neither. A hidden camera in his briefcase recorded it all. We were surrounded outside on the beach by a dozen armed agents. Inside, I had a captive audience and I wanted to host a seminar on Rubens; I hadn't taught one in fifteen years since Princeton. I was in heaven. The drama got the better of me. The crooks presented a manilla envelope. Out came the oil sketch, *Aurora*, wrapped in a red rag. I turned to the ringleader, Orly Beigel, and said, "This is no way to wrap a Rubens." Then I began lecturing them about the painting, the iconography, the style. No question, it was the original stolen from La Coruña's museum. Agent Blair was getting hot under the collar (I later learned that the agents on the beach listening in were none too pleased about my captive seminar). But they got me out, the agents swooped in, arrests were made. Special Agent Zach Mann called it "the picture-perfect takedown." I had been paid—in advance, upon arrival at headquarters—five hundred dollars for the assignment. As the agent peeled off ten crisp fifty-dollar bills, I asked, "You're treasury department. Shouldn't I get a check?" He replied, "Most of the people we do business with prefer cash."

A year later, I flew down to testify at the trial in federal court. Upon arrival the US Attorney told me there was a big problem: The defense had withdrawn their stipulation agreeing that the seized painting was the stolen original from Spain; they were arguing that it was either a fake or a copy, in which case there would be no crime. I now had to convince the jury that the picture seized was beyond doubt an original Rubens, the stolen art. (If its authenticity was in any doubt, the defendants would walk.) By coincidence, I had just come off of jury duty myself in New York the week before, so I knew what jurors needed to hear; they did not want eye-glazing technicalities. After a testy cross-examination, the judge asked the two best questions that clinched the case. First, he wanted to know how certain I was of the authenticity. I replied that I recognized the painting with more certainty than my own children. When he followed up and asked the basis of that certainty, what my methodology was, I looked at the jury, which didn't know Rubens from the deli sandwich, and replied, "It's exactly the same experience, your honor, that we all have when a stack of mail arrives, and we flip through it, and we see we have a letter from Mom. We haven't looked at the return address on the back, haven't opened the letter. How do we know? We recognize the handwriting on the envelope. It's as simple as that. I recognize Rubens's handwriting." The jurors nodded.

The defendants were convicted; the painting was returned to Spain. Special Agent D'Amato was honored by the king of Spain. I got a "Yorktown Certificate" awarded by the treasury department. (After the presentation, my six-year-old-son, Chris, was locked in a holding cell, for experience.) I lived to see forty.

In 2002, I flew down to Miami for a reunion with my favorite Special Agents to film the BBC-Bravo documentary *The Rubens*

Robbers, which—in a coincidence I still cannot fathom—aired and concluded just minutes before Julius Held's memorial service in 2003. Four years later Sky TV came to my apartment to film a sequel, *Miami Sting*, for The Arts Channel. I prefer the first one (I was younger). After two decades of giving art history lectures at the Met Museum, I decided to cap them with a recounting of the best Walter Mitty adventure of a lifetime, complete with video clips for "Rubens Meets Miami Vice." I could never dream up an encore for this sellout. I'm still waiting.

At this very time up at Scribners, new discoveries gave our program in crime-mystery-detective novels a huge boost: major authors signed up and edited by Susanne Kirk, who had been presiding over our mystery list for the past decade. Having taken over in 1980 upon Elinor Parker's retirement, Susanne published not only her inherited British authors Simon Brett, Sheila Radley, and Dorothy Simpson, but also brought on board the prolific Robert Barnard, who would hold the all-time record for mystery novelists at Scribners. In fact, with forty-four Scribner books to his credit, he ranks top among *all* our authors; Rudyard Kipling takes the silver.

In 1990, Susanne brought to the house the biggest bestseller of all: Patricia Cornwell, with the first of her "Kay Scarpetta" crime novels, *Postmortem*, winner of the 1991 Edgar Award for best first novel, soon followed by a parade of winners. Susanne's subsequent discoveries—Janet Evanovich and Kathy Reichs, among others—put Scribners at the top of mystery publishers. By the end of her twenty-nine years with us, no mystery editor in the business could claim a more successful or distinguished list.

The next year, 1991, Matt Bruccoli gave me a commission—in art, not literature. His "authorized" edited and annotated edition of *The Great Gatsby* was about to be published by Cambridge University Press—with our cooperation—and he wanted to distribute a Fitzgerald keepsake to mark its debut. Matt had recently discovered and bought in a rural Pennsylvania antique shop a folio of artwork that he recognized as related to Francis Cugat's famous *Gatsby* cover. He sent me photos and asked for my opinion. I said they were without question the artist's preparatory sketches for that iconic painting, which I had given to Princeton in 1984.

Matt then asked whether I would write an article about them explaining their sequence and role in its creation. I was happy to oblige. It would be an adventure trying to piece together the order and meaning of those sketches, tying them to imagery in Fitzgerald's as-yet-unwritten novel. (In this rare exception, the cover art preceded the finished manuscript.) The result was an article I titled "Celestial Eyes: From Metamorphosis to Masterpiece." Matt published it as an illustrated brochure for the book launch; it was later reprinted in the *Princeton University Library Chronicle*, and finally in the *Playbill* for the Metropolitan Opera's premiere of John Harbison's opera *The Great Gatsby* at the end of the decade. It was the only time my publishing and art history tracks crossed—and the only time I have written a scholarly piece on twentieth-century art.

Following the publication of my father's memoir, I encouraged him to publish a collection of his essays. I had two boxes of his writings—speeches and articles—in my office. By then, he had a neighboring office in the Macmillan Building on Third. The Scribner downtown offices had been vacated in the fall of 1987; the imprints were now all together in one place. I sent Max's desk, briefly mine, down to Princeton for the university librarian's office, where it remains today. The Scribner move downtown lasted only three years. Karen Day and her reference department were now just a few floors below us, so I was able to visit her more often. Karen was enthusiastic about being the publisher of my father's new book and assigned Ann Leslie Tuttle to be its editor. Ann Leslie did a brilliant job of reweaving those pieces into a seamless sequence of thematic chapters with my dad's intriguing titles: "Confessions of a Book Publisher," "The Secret of Being Ernest (and the Secret of Keeping Ernest)," "The Heuristic Power of

Writing," "The Joys of Learning," "Proustian Remembrances," and so forth. The publication was scheduled for June 1993.

I wrote a long introduction explaining the genesis of the book. I also included many of my father's letters to me as a student at St. Paul's, which the school's alumni magazine later reprinted as an article titled "*In Loco Parentis:* Letters from Home." At the end, the book was supplemented by a sampling of short newspaper columns he had dictated for his good friend and neighbor Malcom Forbes's New Jersey newspaper, the *Hills-Bedminster Press.* My mother had served as his loving scribe and then preserved the columns for a second life in print. The inspired title, *In the Web of Ideas*, was my father's, referring to his "life of the mind." Once completed, the book revealed to me an intellectual structure that was both organic and architectural—"a web of ideas" indeed. When I asked Dad how he saw himself therein ("Are you the spider or the fly?"), his response was deliberately Delphic: He declined to be pinned down.

Two months before my father's last book came out, Scribners published its first Pulitzer Prize–winning novel since Hemingway's *The Old Man and the Sea* three decades earlier: Annie Proulx's *The Shipping News*. Along with that coveted prize, the next year brought still more arresting news. Macmillan (along with Scribners) was sold to Paramount Communications, the parent company of Simon & Schuster. A month later, in March, Sumner Redstone's company Viacom won a takeover battle to acquire Paramount. A new imprint of Simon & Schuster, we were now a branch of the Hollywood entertainment industry.

CHAPTER 14

Curator of Classics

JUNE 1994 MARKED THE ARRIVAL OF TWO NEW EDITORS IN charge of Scribners for the new owners, Simon & Schuster, and its new parent company, Viacom: Susan Moldow as publisher, and Nan Graham as editor-in-chief. The first change that the new team made to our century-old "Charles Scribner's Sons" was to edit it down to a singular—and gender-neutral—imprint: "Scribner." For the next and final decade at the firm I would see that imprint flourish yet again. I had first met Susan fifteen years earlier while running subsidiary rights at Scribners when she was an acquiring editor for Walter Meade at Avon. The roster of new Scribner authors would include Frank McCourt (*Angela's Ashes*), Amy Hempel, Don DeLillo, Stephen King, and Pulitzer Prize winner Anthony Doerr. Today Nan is their publisher as well as editor.

For that first year of new ownership, we remained at the old Macmillan Building on Third. I moved downstairs to a new office, my fifth in that building within a decade. It is my only office preserved on film (and YouTube), thanks to the 1994 BBC documentary on Edith Wharton, *A Lady Does Not Write*. The camera crew came that fall to film me on the subject of our most famous female author before we traveled uptown to film Louis Auchincloss in his Park Avenue library. His second Scribner book, *The Style's the*

Man: Reflections on Proust, Fitzgerald, Wharton, Vidal, and Others—classic Louis at his most incisive—followed later that season. Those essays signified a shift in my own role during the coming decade. My chief responsibility would be overseeing the editions (and managing the estates) of our classic authors—Hemingway, Fitzgerald, Wharton, Wolfe—and P. D. James, who was still very much alive and well. That year also marked an unfortunate loss for the Fitzgerald Estate and the "authorized editions" published by Cambridge and us: the resignation of Matt Bruccoli as Fitzgerald editor and trustee.

Matt was a force of nature, as well as the most prolific professor I have ever known, with over fifty books on Fitzgerald, Hemingway, Cozzens, Dickey, Nabokov, and others to his credit by the time of his death in 2008. During his reediting of *Gatsby* in 1990, he was at loggerheads with the other trustees—Fitzgerald's granddaughter Eleanor Lanahan in particular—over his proposed changes to the text mentioned earlier: "retinas" to "irises," "Astoria" to "Long Island City," and so forth. He was often brutal in his rebuffs to Bobbie (Eleanor), whom he considered—with a dose of chauvinism—wholly unqualified to question his editorial expertise. Two decades earlier, Bobbie had illustrated a whimsical children's book, *The Zowbinger*, for Scribners; no doubt that was how he still viewed her: as artistic Zelda's granddaughter. I tried to mediate, to smooth things over. I respected Matt's position with final say as official editor; at the same time, I agreed with the other trustees' reluctance to make changes to the author's text of such an established classic.

I offered to consult with eminent Princeton professor Thomas P. Roche, who had made his name as textual editor of Edmund Spenser's *The Faerie Queene*, several centuries removed from this fray. He was also my favorite English professor as an undergraduate, taught my favorite course (Shakespeare), and remained a close friend; we sat together each Sunday in the Princeton Chapel at what he dubbed "the drunkards' Mass"—at 4:45 p.m. (After

Saturday night parties, it was hard for many of us to wake up on Sunday morning.) Tom agreed with Bobbie: The text should not be altered; any prescribed changes should be relegated to the footnotes. That was the compromise struck, but it didn't last. Against all my pleadings not to resign in anger—this project, after all, was the culmination of Matt's long career as the reigning Fitzgerald scholar—he did just that. The estate then picked Tom Roche to replace him as trustee; Matt's former Fitzgerald graduate student Professor James West III took over as editor. Over the next twenty-five years, Jim would complete the Cambridge Fitzgerald editions—eighteen volumes in all. In an ironic twist, I learned that Tom Roche and Matt had been roommates their freshman year at Yale in 1949 by chance, not choice. They could not have been more different—think *The Odd Couple* with Walter Matthau and Jack Lemmon—but I was fond of them both.

Scribners finally moved out of the Macmillan Building in the summer of 1995 to Rockefeller Center, just one block west of the Scribner Building on Fifth. Because of its landmark status, the gilded "Charles Scribner's Sons" with Scribner lamp on the facade and our name on the southern wall (see jacket art), spelled out in colored bricks, could not be changed; I often called it my "tombstone on Fifth." I loved our new location near the skating rink where my mother would often practice before performing in shows with Ice Theatre of New York. Once I ran into a cousin who was talking with one of the guards in Rock Plaza overlooking the rink. He pointed out my mother on the ice and, to tease me, asked him: "How old would you say that figure skater is?"

The guard replied, "Oh, I think she's more mature than the others; I'd say around fifty."

Smiling, I said to him, "No, I'm fifty. She's my mother."

Our most famous novels soon appeared in a new line of quality paperbacks called "Scribner Paperback Fiction," a reprise of my father's "Scribner Library" thirty-five years earlier. The hardcovers were then rebranded and repackaged (with color jackets) as "Scribner Classics." In a delicious turn of history, these classics now included titles originally published by other houses since Simon & Schuster decided to consolidate and "rebaptize" Macmillan and Atheneum titles as "Scribner." (One can only imagine Kaplan's and Knopf's reactions.) So *Gone with the Wind* now bore our imprint, as did John Knowles's *A Separate Peace*, my favorite of all novels assigned in English class at St. Paul's. My uncle Ned was the model for one of its characters; he and Knowles had been at Exeter summer school during the war, the source of the novel. My Princeton pal Richard Parker starred as Gene in the 1972 film, the first in his Hollywood career as "Parker Stevenson." I sent him an inscribed copy of "our" new classic.

P. D. James's nine Scribner novels joined our new series of paperback classics. We took back the mass-market reprint licenses when they expired in order to publish the titles ourselves, just as my father had done for Hemingway forty years earlier. Today mass-market paperbacks play a distant second to the quality paperback imprints. My father's preference had finally become industry practice.

Dad would have been delighted. But he died in November 1995 on Armistice Day. For the previous two years he had suffered from recurring pneumonia as a result of a neurological illness that caused distorted eyesight, disorientation in space and time, short-term memory loss, and problems swallowing. But his higher intellect remained intact thanks to a pioneering operation in 1993—the first omental transposition to the brain performed in America. He retained his stoic equanimity to the end. The surgeon who performed that operation, Dr. Harry Goldsmith, came to our attention when Scribner editor Ned Chase, father of the comedian Chevy, brought up at an editorial meeting Harry's manuscript for a book on the cover-up of President Roosevelt's mortal illness in 1944 prior to the convention that nominated him for his fourth term. We did not sign up Harry's book, but Ned urged me to introduce him to my dad, who soon became his brave patient for this dangerous but successful operation, later written up in a medical journal of neuroscience. Dad's commitment to the history of science remained unshakable. He practiced what he published.

My father's funeral at St. Bartholomew's, with mourners filling the vast Byzantine church, was a reunion with so many publishing associates over the decades as we thanked them at the door. There was no eulogy; my father forbade it. He said to me shortly before he died, "No eulogy. I'll be listening; if you disobey, you'll hear from me!" The *New York Times* obituary was lovelier than I could have imagined; I was sorry he couldn't read it. But then he had always had little use for dwelling on that page. To those who began the day citing an obituary, he would reply, "People are dying these days who never died before."

A month afterward, the first volume of John Delaney's *Documentary History of Charles Scribner's Sons* was published in the *Dictionary of Literary Biography*. The publisher? Matt Bruccoli's reference company Bruccoli, Clark, Layman. At the time, Matt was editing his own Scribner book, *The Only Thing That Counts: The Ernest Hemingway/Maxwell Perkins Correspondence*, scheduled for the next year, 1996, the Scribner sesquicentennial as well as the Fitzgerald centennial. Matt dedicated the book to our 150th anniversary and, closer to home, in memory of my father. That rich volume of letters back and forth between editor and author calls to mind the most moving—of the 350 I was answering—condolence letter I received. It was from Michael Pietsch and described his experience editing Hemingway with my dad. He said that when he brought his proposed flap copy for review—it was über-Hemingway in its economy of prose—my father praised it but added, "Michael, writing doesn't consist just of what you leave out." (He then added some "thoughtful superlatives," Michael recalled.) I have treasured that letter for the past twenty-seven years.

We celebrated our sesquicentennial with posters and a special issue of a revived *Scribner's Magazine* featuring the original, century-old cover by Maxfield Parrish illustrating a beautiful female personification of autumn silhouetted against a huge sun and holding an abundance of ripe fruit. Picture perfect for the future, as much as for the celebration of our past. A new best-seller would hit the list the next autumn: *Angela's Ashes* by Frank McCourt, followed over the next two years by Don DeLillo's *Underworld* (1997) and Stephen King's first of many Scribner bestsellers, *Bag of Bones* (1998). Down at Princeton, our anniversary was capped by a major exhibition—of rare books, letters, manuscripts, artwork, and portraits—mounted by John Delaney at Firestone Library: *The Company of Writers: Charles Scribner's Sons, 1846–1996*. No other American publishing company has been honored with a show of such treasures. There are, after all, rewards for donating everything, holding back nothing. John's exhibition catalog would prove invaluable for my writing this history: He provided the timeline.

Another anniversary was looming on the horizon: Hemingway's centennial. For the poster, I chose a sentence from *A Moveable Feast*: "All you have to do is write one true sentence." I wanted to celebrate it with an exhibition and a major publication. In my father's 1974 volume *The Enduring Hemingway* I found an excerpt titled "Miss Mary's Lion" from a large, unpublished Hemingway manuscript based on his 1954 safari, which included two near-fatal plane crashes. It was known as his *African Journal*. With his son Patrick Hemingway's support, I contacted the JFK Library and requested a copy of the manuscript. After reading it, I was convinced that with proper editing it could be as good a book as *The Dangerous Summer*.

I proposed to Patrick, who had lived in Africa for decades and accompanied his father on that safari, that he serve as principal editor; eventually I convinced him and he forged ahead. But he would need a skilled Scribner editor with whom to collaborate. I knew just the one: Gillian Blake, a young and gifted editor who had recently worked with Matt on his volume on the

Hemingway-Perkins correspondence and with Bobby Kennedy on *The Riverkeepers*. Whenever I brought in a book, I turned it over to Gillian, always with brilliant results. She and Patrick turned out a revealing and lyrical book with an evocative title: *True at First Light*. Today she is the editor-in-chief and publisher at Crown Books; among her catalog of best-selling authors are Pulitzer Prize winner Elizabeth Kolbert, Rachel Maddow, Matthew McConaughey, and Michelle Obama, just to mention a few minor stars. Like Michael Pietsch, Gillian is a most illustrious alum. Both edited Hemingway.

The upcoming Hemingway centennial in 1999 brought a film crew to our offices in October 1997. Hemingway's granddaughter Mariel was planning to narrate a film on her grandfather for the A&E television series *Biography*, and her husband, director Steve Crisman, asked to film me with observations on his life with Scribners and my family. I almost canceled the day before; I had been hit with a family health crisis over the weekend and felt too rattled to face a camera. Steve persuaded me to let them come and film me anyway; he said it would prove therapeutic, and added, "We can discuss your problem afterwards. We in the Hemingway family have some experience in these matters." He was so right. For the hour of filming I felt transported back to the days of father and grandfather; on an impulse I read aloud the condolence letter about my grandfather that Hemingway had written to my dad. It required no acting; it brought me close to tears and was included in the final cut. Written by the young and gifted Tom Folsom, that short documentary remains the best portrait of the artist on film. It would be eclipsed in length and press coverage two decades later by the Ken Burns three-part series for PBS. But Folsom and Crisman captured in an hour and a half what eluded Burns in six hours: the essence of the writer. Less is more, especially for Hemingway.

In 1998, our publishing imprint was bifurcated by the imminent sale of Simon & Schuster's education and reference divisions. Scribner Reference, headed by Karen Day, was being sold to Pearson. Unlike the trade books, our reference books continued to be published under our original trademark, "Charles Scribner's Sons." I wanted to ensure that those books, my father's legacy, would continue to carry that imprint long after the sale. Karen was worried that Simon & Schuster might not permit it. So I called the president of the education division and followed up with a faxed memo explaining why it was so important to me personally and to my father's legacy that when the sale was completed our original trademark should go to the new corporate owners of the reference books, the "crown jewels." If the top brass at Simon & Schuster's trade division, my bosses, had gotten word of my secret intervention it would have been the end of me there, and I couldn't blame them. But I felt I owed it to my father and to history to preserve our full name. It all worked out. The trade-marks "Charles Scribner's Sons" and "Scribners" would thereafter be owned by the reference publisher, who would grant a perpetual license to Simon & Schuster permitting the name "Scribner" to be used on their trade books. My colleagues at Scribner were both baffled and indignant upon learning of that corporate decision upstairs; I shrugged and kept my silence.

The next summer, his last at St. Paul's, our son Charlie went to work for Karen Day at Charles Scribner's Sons. He would continue in that summer job for the next three years. I had given Karen two of my father's chairs dating back to the founder for her office at Thomson Gale, the new corporate owners. They carried their own upholstered—if silent—history of famous sitters in our company of authors. The other two I kept with the desk, now in the Scribner Library at Firestone in Princeton. Charlie went to work on *The Encyclopedia of the Renaissance*; one of his tasks was to oversee the article on Rubens that I had been commissioned to write for it—three years after a similar Rubens entry I contributed to the *Encyclopedia Britannica*. His job was to nudge dilatory con-tributors; his dad needed no nudging. I'm pleased to discover that both are still in print (Rubens is evidently not high on the list for revisionists). Three years later, Charlie would contribute his own article to a Scribner reference series by writing the biography of all-time football and hockey star Hobey Baker (St. Paul's/Princeton) for the *Scribner Encyclopedia of American Lives: Sports Volume*. He also edited the *Encyclopedia of Food and Culture*.

During the summer of the Hemingway centennial, I took part in a panel discussion in Oyster Bay, New York, filmed by C-SPAN, together with Patrick Hemingway and Lillian Ross. Seated next to me at dinner afterward, she told me how much she had admired and liked my grandfather, the man she had so cruelly mocked in her *New Yorker* piece half a century earlier. Time is the ultimate revisionist. That fall, I concluded the centennial celebrations with an exhibition at Firestone Library, another mounted by curator John Delaney. Six weeks later, son Charlie got his letter of admission—the first sixth-generation namesake in unbroken succession at that university. (Perhaps our next Charles, my grandson, will show more originality.) At Scribners, we concluded negotiations on a new contract for the Hemingway books, adding another decade to our exclusive publishing rights. It would later be extended for the life of copyright, but not by me. As the millennium approached, I could see that it would soon be time to move on.

The last Hemingway event I took an official part in was the memorial service for his eldest son, Jack, at the Explorers Club in New York in December 2000. There I saw Mariel and Steve Crisman for the last time. Mariel and I gave eulogies for this superb sportsman and son, to whom, as a child, his father had dedicated *The Sun Also Rises*. In my brief talk, I said that I felt a special kinship with Jack; though a generation apart, we were both the eldest of three sons. But far more than that, we identified as "professional sons." Upon turning fifty, my father had quipped to his sons, "I feel as though my life is almost half over." At the same milestone, Jack told my father, "I've spent the first fifty years of my life being my father's son, and will spend the next fifty being my daughters' father."

Those words rang true. A few weeks earlier I had been sitting at breakfast at the Ivy Club in Princeton while visiting my freshman son. Hearing my name mentioned, a girl looked up from her reading and asked with all the eagerness of youth, "Oh, are you Charlie Scribner's *father*?" For years at that table I had been "Charlie Scribner's *son*." My dad was the real one, a university trustee. Now the table was turned. (Years earlier at our Scribner offices, whenever I picked up my phone and the caller asked to speak with "Mr. Scribner," I would reply, "Do you want the real one or his son?") At the end of the service, the great pianist Byron Janis—married to the daughter of Hemingway's pal Gary Cooper—played the same waltz I had played two decades earlier for Scottie Fitzgerald in my office. But now it fit the occasion to perfection: Chopin's *Adieu* waltz.

The one book I tried—and failed—to win for Scribners was Jacques Barzun's magnum opus, *From Dawn to Decadence*. His longtime publisher Harper had the upper hand, and deservedly. They could afford to outbid us since they had a backlist of his books that would benefit from sales of the new one. Who was I to argue against continuity? Jacques had retired several years earlier and was now living in Texas. He sent me his section on Renaissance and Baroque artists for suggestions; I was as happy as honored to oblige. In return, he gave me too generous an acknowledgment and—even more surprising—referred the reader to my *Rubens* and *Bernini* as "the books to read." Soon after its publication, I ran into attorney Peter Megargee Brown, father of literary agent and childhood friend Blair Brown, at a local restaurant. He called me over to his table and asked, "Do you realize you are the only author with *two* books recommended in Barzun's *Dawn to Decadence*?" (It was news to me; I was impressed that he kept score—and that he had read the whole book.) "Well, don't be too surprised. He edited both of them," I replied.

By the new millennium the biggest name on our list of best-sellers was Stephen King, who had been lured away from Viking three years earlier. By this time, our younger son, Christopher, was a teenager—old enough now to come to my rescue. One day during school vacation, I brought him to the office. He played on my computer while I was on the phone, my back turned to the door. I heard a voice, looked around briefly and saw a middle-aged man wearing a work shirt and jeans, and said—a bit too brusquely—"I'm sorry, I'm on the phone, I'll be with you soon." He disappeared down the hall and Chris piped up, "Dad, that was *Stephen King* you just blew off."

So I raced down the hall and caught up with King. I apologized for not realizing who he was, then spotted the gold medal of the Virgin Mary around his neck and complimented him, "I'm so glad to see you're wearing the Blessed Virgin medal."

He replied, "Well, I'm not actually Catholic—I just like it."

"That doesn't matter," I said in turn. "I just think it's a great idea with the books you write."

The year 2000 brought back into my life the only soprano we had ever published—Elisabeth Schwarzkopf, my musical standard and, some might say, obsession. That fall I got a fax from her out of the blue. I had last seen her fifteen years before at a party hosted by the widow of author John Gunther. Dame Elisabeth—she had been knighted in the meantime by Queen Elizabeth—wrote to me explaining that she was working with a writer on a possible memoir and she would like to have permission to quote from her book *On and Off the Record*. That brought back memories of the 1981 Frankfurt Book Fair, where I was in charge of taking care of her as she met with a host of foreign publishers at our booth. I faxed back that of course she could use anything she wanted, but she had given me an idea: I'd like to have the book republished in paperback. There was only one problem—we didn't have her original photos needed for the illustrations. Did she still have them?

After several more faxes, including photos of us together at the Frankfurt Book Fair, she concluded that they were not to be found. So she mailed to me a file of new photos covering her life with her late husband, classical record impresario Walter Legge, the subject—and chief author—of the book. He had been signed up to write his autobiography but died shortly thereafter, and this book was the result: a collection of his writings, introduced by his wife. I made my selection of photos and then Elisabeth asked me to compose the captions in her voice, first-person singular—or singer. That was a heady assignment; I've never had a better one, my sole stint as a ghost writer. It was also my final editorial project at Scribner; I could not have chosen a better one to assign myself. The book was published anew (by Northeastern University Press) as my days in publishing were drawing to a close.

At the same time, I was briefly tempted to write a foreword to the new Scribner Classics edition of Martin Buber's *I and Thou [Ich und Du]* that I was overseeing for reissue. I'm sure my reconnection with Elisabeth, Strauss's consummate Marschallin in *Der Rosenkavalier*—my favorite opera after Mozart's *Figaro*—prompted this idea. She would later tell me, "Everything you need to know about life, about living life, is in *Der Rosenkavalier*." Strauss had been well served by his librettist, Hugo von Hofmannsthal. As I revisited Buber's classic, which I first read at Princeton in Buber scholar Malcolm Diamond's religion course, I was struck by the idea that he might have been influenced by Hofmannsthal's opening dialogue in *Rosenkavalier*.

As the curtain rises at the breaking of dawn, Oktavian sings to his beloved Marschallin: "Du, du! Was heißt das 'Du'? Was 'du und ich'?"

> *You, you! What does "you" mean? What about "you and I"?*
> *Does it make any sense? They are words, empty words! No?*
> *Tell me! But in spite of that, there is something in them, a*
> *delirium, a magnetism, a longing and urging, thirsting and*

burning: as now my hand finds your hand, the desire for you,
the holding of you, I am that that desires you, but the "I" is
lost in the "You."

To me it read like an anticipation of Buber's mystical meditations, written a decade after the premiere of the opera. By the time Buber composed *Ich und Du* in Vienna, *Der Rosenkavalier* was already famous. I tried to find some firm connection between Hofmannsthal and Buber—there was some evidence that Buber admired his poetry—but I came up with nothing specific. Perhaps the influence of the playwright/poet on the Jewish theologian was subconscious. In any event, it was never publicly acknowledged. I decided not to write that foreword. So I write it now in my book, not his.

I stayed for three more years, working mainly on my own book, a spiritual journal I called *Epiphanies*; it would later be titled *The Shadow of God: A Journey Through Memory, Art, and Faith*. I started writing this journal—the first in my life—on Epiphany 2002, onward to Epiphany 2003. I saw it as a private exercise for myself, not for publication: two typed pages per day. By the time I finished, I thought there might be enough material (730 pages) from which an editor might carve out a book. When the time had come to seek advice on the completed journal, I turned to Doubleday. Their line of Catholic books, Image Books, was second to none. I knew the religion editor from twenty years back when I was looking for one at Macmillan. But he had returned to England. Had they found a successor? Yes. His name? "Michelle Rapkin." Back to the future, again. This was a coincidence too good to ignore.

When my book was edited and published in 2006, Doubleday arranged for an interview with the largest Catholic TV network in the world, EWTN. But it was canceled just days before the taping date. When I asked why, I was informed that the ultra-conservative board had read the book and decided it was "not

Catholic enough." I took it as a compliment. Fortunately a more ecumenical Catholic program (*Christopher Closeup*) invited me on their show, and I've never enjoyed an interview more. By the time that series wrapped in 2012, it had had one of the longest runs at that time in television history: fifty-five years. I'd been a judge and presenter for the Christopher Awards for several years, long after accompanying as a young editor our Scribner winners, beginning with Loren Eiseley. The Christophers' famous motto is "It's better to light one candle than to curse the darkness." The title of my book came from a Latin inscription my father gave me my last year in college as I began writing my thesis: *Lux umbra Dei*—"light is the shadow of God." No wonder that Christophers interview felt so fitting.

Three years earlier, my manuscript completed, I knew it was time to forge ahead with my own book and say farewell to Rockefeller Center. The big anniversaries had been celebrated, my father honored, and the Scribner imprint would indeed "fare well" for years to come. I kept my desk there for six months after I was officially off the payroll (as my father had at Macmillan). Then, one day in June 2004, I was working at it and heard there was a retirement party in the boardroom down the hall—for Susanne Kirk. For the past fourteen years, she had been brilliantly managing her roster of mystery and crime writers from her home in Mississippi, traveling up to Rockefeller Center every six weeks. (Those were still the days of faxes, phones, and UPS; no working from home "remotely"; it was just remote.)

I joined the festive celebration for our star editor, who had joined the company the same year as I—1975. In my impromptu words of tribute to this dear friend and colleague of twenty-nine years, I ended by saying, as much to my own surprise as those in the room, "If you are moving on, Susanne, I'm joining you. This will be my last month." I sent my furniture, the founder's, down to Princeton. I was going home—to travel on the other track.

Epilogue

The Sons Also Rise

Two weeks after I left Scribners for good, our most famous novel was serialized in the *New York Times*: *The Great Gatsby*—in full and for free. My father and I would never have permitted that. We both were always reluctant to allow competing versions of our prize books. Hemingway's longtime lawyer, Alfred Rice, once put it to me: "Charlie, never let your prize racehorse out of the stable except to run in the big races with the big purses." But that serialization proved the right decision; it cost no sales of the book and, like that free paperback edition to our troops at the end of the Second World War, it boosted interest in Fitzgerald even more. Ritchie and I went to an event that week at Borders Books on Columbus Circle to hear Sam Waterston and his actress daughter Elisabeth read from *Gatsby*. (They were starring together in a summer production of my favorite Shakespeare play, *Much Ado About Nothing*.) It was a revelation: Waterston, the definitive Nick Carraway thirty years earlier in the film, had us all chuckling as he read "his" narrative. I had never before caught the wit and humor in that classic book; all four Gatsby films (1949, 1974, 2000, 2013) treated it with stately reverence. Classics can do that. Fitzgerald, on the other hand, could be funny. That was an epiphany for the ears.

A decade later, I would run into Woody Allen in the lobby of our Paris hotel, the Bristol. I told him that I wished he had made a film of *Gatsby*. (The Baz Luhrmann film the year before, starring Leonardo DiCaprio, was a brilliant "grand rap opera" production worthy of Zeffirelli but without Fitzgerald's humor.) Woody would have translated the humor onto the screen better than anyone, I argued, citing his recent *Midnight in Paris*. He replied that it was the one novel he had always wanted to film, "but others got there first." Our loss. He left me a nice letter with the concierge, and that, I thought, was the end of it. But a few years later, I watched *A Rainy Day in New York*, his last film set in the United States, starring Timothée Chalamet as a young man named . . . *Gatsby*! I can't help wondering. To date, the most faithful—if least known—adaptation of Fitzgerald's masterpiece is the 2000 A&E film starring Toby Stephens, Mira Sorvino, and Paul Rudd. Stephens made the perfect Gatsby, with flashes of the gangster beneath a suave veneer. Perhaps it takes a British actor to capture that duality; it surely doesn't hurt to have Dame Maggie Smith as the actor's mother.

The next Feast of the Epiphany, in 2005, I began a second journal titled *Home by Another Route*. The title referred to "Journey of the Magi," my favorite poem by T. S. Eliot, which I had first read in school. But it may also have been inspired by the story I had been told about our author Tillich speaking at our author Buber's funeral in 1965. Tillich concluded his eulogy saying that we all seek and approach the same God, but by different routes. My journal would be published a decade later by Paulist Press— after Michelle edited those 730 pages down to a 140-page book with large type and small trim size and illustrated by my favorite Renaissance painting at the Met: Sassetta's *Journey of the Magi*. It concluded with my own pilgrimage a few weeks after Epiphany 2006: a visit to Dame Elisabeth Schwarzkopf in Schruns, Austria, where the young Hemingway, between ski runs, completed *The Sun Also Rises* nine decades earlier.

After the past several years of corresponding via fax and phone calls, I had longed to visit Elisabeth again in person. In a gracious response to my Bernini book, she wrote back that it called to mind all those years in the EMI recording studios with her husband, "sculpting in sound." I now wanted to discuss with her at length her views on that sculpting, in which she was my prime candidate for "the Bernini of vocal artistry." The editor of *Opera News* commissioned me to write an article about her, which would be titled "The Voice of Mozart," for their upcoming issue celebrating the composer's 250th anniversary, his *bicenquinquage-nary*—a term I had discovered at Princeton's celebration ten years before.

The pilgrimage to that skiing village in the Vorarlberg took only two planes and *six* trains from the Zurich airport. The fourth of those trains had "The Ernest Hemingway" emblazoned on its cars. I knew, with relief, I was on the right track. I brought along a leather-bound diary that had remained pristine ever since Ritchie gave it to me as a wedding gift in 1979, the year Elisabeth's husband died and she retired from the concert stage. I taped my sessions with her over the next two days and then each evening at the Hemingway Inn (I kid you not) I recorded my impressions in that diary. The resulting article was published in July; I mailed Elisabeth a copy and held my breath. A week later she called and said that of all the profiles written of her over the years this one was her favorite. She then, despite her aversion to digital record-ings, gave me permission to issue a DVD of the 1963 television broadcast of her "Viennese Evening" with conductor-violinist Willi Boskovsky. That was the last time I spoke with her; two weeks later she died in her sleep at the age of ninety. I wrote an introduction to the VAI disc as my memorial tribute.

Two years later, I translated from the German (keeping up with Dad) a beautiful photobiography, *Elisabeth Schwarzkopf: From Flower Maiden to Marschallin*, by Kirsten Liese, who later commissioned me to translate her book *Wagnerian Heroines*. I arranged for the Schwarzkopf book to be published in America and the United Kingdom, most fittingly by Amadeus Press, and added as an epilogue the full version of my "Voice of Mozart." On saying goodbye in Schruns to Elisabeth, who had just finished an impromptu session coaching me at the piano, she asked, "Why do you want to *write* about music when you can *make* it?" I returned home to both keyboards.

When my English version of the Schwarzkopf book was complete, I sent it to a copyeditor for final polishing. By a coincidence worthy of Einstein's maxim ("God's way of remaining anonymous"), she turned out to be the very one who had copyedited my dad's memoir two decades earlier. More recently, she had written a superb article for the entry on my dad in Oxford's *American National Biography*, their successor to our *Dictionary of American Biography*. Once again, as Fitzgerald wrote, "If it wasn't life, it was magnificent."

This book is about Scribners, not my life post Scribner. But the dialogue between time past and time present would continue in the years ahead. Our elder son, Charlie, married his Princeton sweetheart, Elizabeth Yates, in 2006 in Birmingham, Alabama; they first met at St. Paul's School. He got his MPA from the University of Alabama at Birmingham and is executive director of Black Warrior Riverkeeper, a branch of his old mentor Bobby Kennedy's Waterkeeper Alliance. Elizabeth got her PhD in mathematics at University of Alabama at Birmingham and is a banker. Among the four children under their roof are a Blair and a Charles.

After graduating from Georgetown, our younger son, Christopher, went to work in the US Senate, earned a master's in journalism, and joined Teach for America in Huntsville, Alabama. A graduate of Vanderbilt Law School, he was admitted to the New York Bar in 2020; his wife, Lauren Cook, is also an attorney. The first Charles Scribner wanted to be a lawyer but had to choose a different path; his thrice-great-grandson fulfilled that original calling.

Looking back, I recall a favorite saying of my father's by French philosopher Montaigne. Let him have the last word: "I have no more made my book than my book has made me."

ACKNOWLEDGMENTS

This history and memoir of our family publishing house, known for most of its life as "Charles Scribner's Sons," began as a talk I gave in October 1978 at the Rowfant Club in Cleveland. That club of enthusiastic bibliophiles later asked me to revise, expand, and edit those remarks for a limited-edition booklet they published seven years later. In 1992 I gave a more informal and personal version in a talk for the Thomas Cooper Society at the University of South Carolina at the invitation of the great Fitzgerald scholar and friend Matthew J. Bruccoli—a version I later published in a special revival issue of *Scribner's Magazine* for our company's sesquicentennial in 1996 as a memorial to my father, who died on Armistice Day in 1995.

That memorial was especially apt since my original talk had been based on an early article he penned in 1957 and titled "A Family Tradition." He later expanded it after dinner one night in a taped conversation peppered with his irreverent wit and delicious sense of irony (I still have the cassette punctuated with my mother's bursts of laughter; she was always his best audience). If plagiarism is the sincerest compliment one can pay, then never was it more richly deserved.

I am most grateful to the following who read drafts of my manuscript and offered invaluable corrections and suggestions: my son Charlie, Brian Regan, Michael Pietsch, Lee Rodgers, Susanne Kirk, Gerard Belliveau, and Michelle Rapkin. Michelle then edited it with her impeccable insight and imagination that left no chapter unimproved. My wife, Ritchie, deserves special thanks for her patient support throughout my manic month of writing.

At Princeton University Library, which houses our publishing and family archives, I wish to thank William G. Noel, Daniel J. Linke, and Sarah J. Logue for their unfailing help and good cheer in making my research in Special Collections a series of homecomings. Special thanks to AnnaLee Pauls for translating our ancient family photos into pristine digital images.

Jed Lyons, Rowman & Littlefield's president and CEO, offered both early encouragement and a preemptive contract for this book before my *Sacred Muse* (Rowman & Littlefield, 2023) was off his press. At Lyons Press, I am indebted to an all-star publishing team: co-editorial director (and fellow Princetonian) Eugene Brissie; managing editor Janice Braunstein; copyeditor Amanda Kirsten; jacket designer Diana Nuhn; and Jason Rossi in marketing. They uphold the best of the tradition.